Paper Trading Boss Battles - Beginner Mode

Bhushan Polepally

Speak Loud Books

First edition 2026

Dedication

To my wife,
for your constant support and encouragement,

and to my niece,
whose bright future reminds me why financial education should start early.

CONTENTS

INTRODUCTION

Warren Buffett bought his first stock when he was eleven years old, and he's said publicly that his only regret was not starting sooner. Meanwhile, the average American doesn't invest a single dollar until the age of thirty-three - handing away over **twenty years** of the most powerful wealth-building force in history: compound growth.

That twenty-year gap is the reason this book exists. If you're between ten and twenty years old and you're holding these pages right now, you have something that billionaires, CEOs, and Wall Street veterans would trade anything to get back. Not money. Not connections. **Time.**

And this book is going to show you exactly how to use it.

The Problem Nobody Talks About

You spend thousands of hours in school learning algebra, memorizing dates, and labeling diagrams of the water cycle. All useful. But somewhere along the way, the education system forgot to teach you the one skill that affects every single day of your adult life: how money actually works.

Nobody explains what the stock market is. Nobody tells you how companies grow or shrink. Nobody shows you why a single dollar invested at age thirteen could be worth five times more than a dollar invested at thirty. By the time most people start thinking about investing, they're already decades behind - and they learn through expensive real-money mistakes, bad advice from social media influencers, or worse, they never learn at all.

And here's the part that should really grab your attention: **you already have the skills to understand the stock market. You just don't know it yet.**

Every time you play Fortnite, you make split-second decisions under pressure, manage limited resources, and adapt your strategy when the situation changes. Every Minecraft world you build requires resource planning, patience, and long-term thinking. Every chess match trains your brain to recognize patterns and think three moves ahead. Every Roblox trade teaches you supply and demand. Every ranked match in any competitive game forces you to deal with losing, adjust your approach, and come back stronger.

You've been training for the stock market your entire gaming life. The controls are just different. This book translates them.

Your Guide Through the Arena

I have an MBA in Finance. I've been actively trading and investing in the U.S. stock market for over fifteen years. I've worked as a financial advisor, helping families and individuals build wealth through smart, disciplined strategies. I've navigated roaring bull markets and survived painful bear markets. I've made great trades, and I've made terrible ones - and I can tell you without hesitation that the losses taught me more than the wins ever did.

But credentials alone don't write a good book for young readers. What sets this book apart is that I didn't write it as a dry finance textbook. I wrote it as someone who understands how your generation learns: through games, through doing, through systems you can explore and master on your own terms.

I've been noticing teenagers for years, and I'm curious about how they take in complex information. And the answer was staring me in the face the entire time. You master complicated games with deep mechanics, layered strategies, and steep learning curves - without anyone handing you a textbook. You learn by playing. You learn by failing. You learn by leveling up.

So I built this book the same way. Every financial concept is mapped to a gaming mechanic you already understand. The stock market is a massive multiplayer arena. Your portfolio is your inventory. Charts are replay footage. Support and resistance are walls and floors. Indicators are power-ups. Your trading plan is your loadout. And by the final chapter, you'll face a Boss Battle that puts everything together.

If you can play a video game, you can learn to trade. That's not a slogan. That's exactly how this book works.

Your Quest: From Level 1 to Boss Battle

Picture this. You've just loaded into a brand-new game. A massive open world stretches out in front of you. Your character has zero experience points, an empty inventory, and a blank world map. The veterans on the server look impossibly far ahead - armored up, loaded out, moving with a confidence you don't yet feel.

That's you right now. Level 1. And that's exactly where every legend begins.

Each chapter of this book is a new level. In the early levels, you'll learn the game's controls - what stocks actually are, how the market moves, and the vocabulary that unlocks everything else. You'll choose your server (a free paper trading platform loaded with $100,000 in virtual cash) and scout the map to pick your first stocks from real U.S. companies like Apple, Nike, Amazon, and Microsoft.

Then the game gets serious. You'll crack open the game engine to understand the hidden forces that push stock prices up and down. You'll pick up your first weapon - candlestick charts - and learn to read them like a chess player reading a board. You'll discover walls and floors (support and resistance levels) that act as invisible boundaries on the battlefield. You'll unlock three power-ups - Moving Averages, Volume, and RSI - that professional traders use every single day.

By Chapter 9, you'll build a complete loadout: a written trading plan with rules for when to buy, when to sell, when to cut your losses, and how much to risk on each trade. Chapter 10 teaches you the hardest skill in the entire game - taking a hit without rage-quitting. Because in this arena, losses aren't game over. They're XP.

And then comes the Boss Battle. Chapter 11 drops you into a structured ten-trade challenge that tests every skill you've built. You'll track your wins, analyze your losses, grade yourself honestly, and walk away with a clear, data-backed picture of exactly who you are as a trader.

The best part? **Zero real money is ever at risk.** Paper trading uses virtual cash with live market data. Every stock price is real. Every chart is real. Every lesson is real. The only thing that's simulated is the money. Think of it as creative mode for the stock market - a practice server where the stakes are zero but the skills you build are one hundred percent transferable to the real thing.

How This Book Is Built

Beginner Mode has eleven chapters, and each one follows the same structure: a core concept taught through gaming analogies you already understand, real-world examples using actual U.S. companies and stock tickers, a hands-on mission at the end that moves you from reading to doing, and a case study showing another young paper trader putting the lesson into practice.

Chapters 1 and 2 build your foundation: what the market is and the vocabulary that unlocks everything. Chapters 3 and 4 get you set up on a platform and picking your first stocks. Chapter 5 reveals why prices move. Chapters 6 through 8 hand you the technical tools: charts, support and resistance, and indicators. Chapter 9 builds your trading plan. Chapter 10 teaches you how to handle losses like a professional. And Chapter 11 is the Boss Battle that ties it all together.

This is Book 1 of a four-book series. Beginner Mode is your starting zone. Book 2 - The Trading Skill Tree - takes you intermediate with sector analysis, financial reports, and advanced position sizing. Book 3 goes advanced. Book 4 tackles trading psychology. And the Companion Journal dashboard gives you templates, scorecards, and tracking tools to use alongside every book.

But none of that matters until you finish Beginner Mode. Every skill tree in every game starts with the same thing: the first point. This is yours.

The Transformation Promise

When you first picked up this book, the stock market might have seemed like a topic reserved for grown-ups. Complicated. Intimidating. Something you'd deal with "someday."

By the time you finish Chapter 11, you'll see the market for what it really is: a skill-based arena where strategy, patience, and discipline win - exactly like the games you already love. You'll look at the companies behind your phone, your sneakers, your favorite apps, and your streaming services, and you'll see them not just as products but as opportunities. You'll understand charts, indicators, and trading plans better than most adults you know. And you'll have a journal full of real paper trades to prove it.

You will go from someone who has never touched the stock market to a confident, disciplined paper trader who understands the U.S. financial system from the inside out.

All without risking a single real dollar.

That's the promise of this book.

Are you ready, Player One?

Let's begin.

Chapter 1

Welcome to the Trading Arena - Your Character Select Screen

You've Been Gaming for Years.

You've built empires in Minecraft that stretch across entire worlds. You've survived sweaty Battle Royale matches in Fortnite when the storm was closing in and you had three hit points left. You've outplayed opponents in chess with moves they never saw coming. You know what it feels like to read a situation, make a decision under pressure, and come out on top.

Imagine if I told you that there's a real-world game where using your skills like strategy, patience, recognizing patterns, and staying calm can actually lead to financial success?

Not someday-when-you're-forty wealthy. We're talking about building a skill right now, as a teenager, that most adults wish they had started learning at your age. A skill that grows more powerful every single year you practice it, like a character that never stops levelling up.

Welcome to the stock market. Welcome to the arena.

And the best part? You can start playing today without risking a single dollar.

The Biggest Multiplayer Game on Earth

Let's start with the basics. What exactly is the stock market?

Think of it like the biggest massively multiplayer online game ever created. Millions of players - from teenagers scrolling their phones to hedge fund managers on Wall Street - log in every single day. They buy, they sell, they strategize, they compete. And instead of trading swords, skins, or Robux, they trade tiny pieces of real companies.

When you buy a **stock** (also called a **share**), you're buying a small slice of ownership in a company. Think about Minecraft. Mojang, the studio that created it, was once a tiny Swedish game company. Microsoft bought Mojang in 2014 for $2.5 billion. If Mojang had been a publicly traded company and you had bought shares when Minecraft was just blowing up, you would have owned a tiny piece of every Minecraft sale, every update, every expansion. As the game got more popular and the company grew, your little piece would have become more and more valuable.

That's essentially how stocks work. Companies are the characters in this game. Stocks are the power-ups that let you share in their success. And the stock market is the giant arena where all of this happens.

The Two Big Game Servers: NYSE and NASDAQ

In the United States, there are two main stock exchanges - think of them as two massive game servers where all the action takes place.

The first is the **NYSE (New York Stock Exchange)**. It's the oldest and largest stock exchange in the world, located on Wall Street in New York City. It's been running since 1792 - think of it as the OG server, the classic arena with centuries of history. The NYSE is home to some of the most well-known companies on the planet: Walmart, Coca-Cola, Johnson & Johnson, and Walt Disney. It's the heavyweight server, known for big, established companies that have been around for decades.

The second server is **NASDAQ**. It's newer, faster, and fully electronic - there's no physical trading floor with people shouting orders. NASDAQ is where the tech giants live. Apple, Microsoft, Amazon, Google (Alphabet), Tesla, Meta, and NVIDIA all trade on NASDAQ. If the NYSE is the classic dungeon-crawling RPG, NASDAQ is the sleek, high-speed esports arena.

Both servers run the same game. Some massive companies, like Berkshire Hathaway, are on the NYSE, while others, like Apple, chose NASDAQ. As a beginner, you don't need to pick sides. You just need to know that this is where the action happens, every weekday from **9:30 AM to 4:00 PM Eastern Time**.

Yes, the market has fixed hours, just like a scheduled tournament match. No late-night grinding here.

The Leaderboards: Dow Jones and S&P 500

Every game has leaderboards, and the U.S. stock market has some famous ones.

The **Dow Jones Industrial Average (the Dow)** tracks just 30 of the biggest, most influential companies in America - think of it as the Top 30 Players leaderboard. Names like Apple, Goldman Sachs, McDonald's, and Nike sit on this list. When the news says "The Dow dropped 400 points today," they're telling you how those 30 giants performed.

The **S&P 500** is a bigger leaderboard. It tracks the top 500 companies in the United States. Most professional traders and investors consider the S&P 500 the true scoreboard of the American stock market. If the Dow is the Top 30 ranked players, the S&P 500 is the full competitive tier list.

You'll hear these names constantly as you learn to trade. For now, just know they're the scoreboards that tell you whether the overall market is having a good day or a rough one.

Why Should a Teenager Care About All This?

Here's a question: if you could start levelling up a character today, and every single day that character got a little stronger, a little richer, a little more powerful - would you wait until you were 30 to start playing?

Of course not. You'd start right now.

That's exactly what learning about the stock market does for you. And the secret weapon that makes starting young so powerful has a name. It's called **compound interest**, and it's the most overpowered mechanic in the entire game of money.

Compound Interest: The XP Multiplier

In most games, your XP (experience points) grows at a steady rate. Defeat an enemy, get 10 XP. Defeat another, get 10 more. Nice and linear.

Compound interest doesn't work like that. It works like a multiplier that keeps getting bigger.

Here's a simple example. Say you invest $1,000 and it grows at 10% per year (which is roughly what the S&P 500 has returned on average over long periods). After one year, you've got $1,100. Cool, but not mind-blowing. But here's the magic - in year two, you earn 10% not just on your original $1,000, but on the full $1,100, thats $1,210 at year 2. Your money starts earning money on its own money.

After 10 years, that $1,000 becomes roughly $2,600. After 20 years, it's about $6,700. After 30 years? Over $17,400. And that's without adding a single extra dollar.

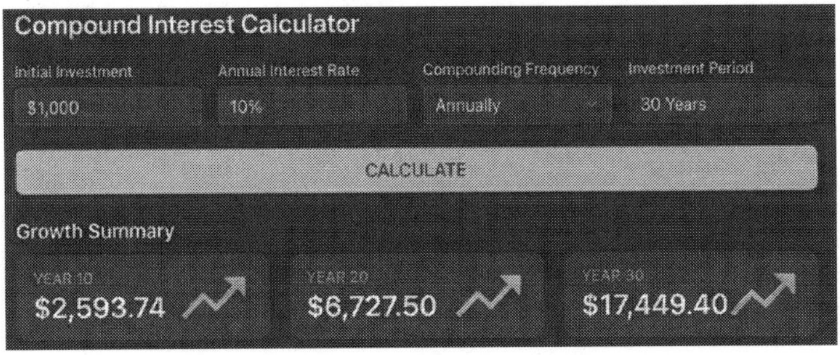

Compounding Growth

Now here's why your age is your superpower. If you start understanding markets at 13, and your friend starts at 25, you have a 12-year head start. Those 12 extra years of compounding are worth more than almost anything your friend can do to catch up. It's like getting a 12-level head start in a game where levels get exponentially harder to gain.

Warren Buffett, the most famous investor in the world, bought his first stock when he was 11 years old. He's said many times that he wishes he had started even earlier. Today, he's worth over $100 billion. That didn't happen overnight - it happened because he started young and let compounding do its thing for over 70 years.

Gamer Tip: In RPGs, early XP gains seem tiny but they unlock the skill trees that make you unstoppable later. Compound interest works the same way. Starting early is the ultimate cheat code.

It's Not Just About Money

Learning about the stock market at your age does something even more valuable than growing money. It teaches you how the world actually works.

When you understand stocks, you start seeing the world differently. That new iPhone everyone's buying? You think about Apple's stock price. Gas prices shooting up? You wonder which energy companies like ExxonMobil might benefit. Nike drops a massive new sneaker collab? You think about what happens to their share price on NASDAQ.

You stop being just a consumer and start thinking like an owner. And that shift in thinking - from consumer to owner - is one of the most powerful upgrades you can give your brain.

Paper Trading: Your Practice Server

Now, I can hear what you're thinking: "But I'm a kid. I don't have money to invest. And even if I did, isn't the stock market risky?"

Fair point. And this is exactly where things get exciting.

Meet **paper trading** - your practice server.

Paper trading is simulated trading. You use everything that's real about the stock market - real stock prices, real market movements, real company news - but you trade with fake money. Virtual currency. Practice V-Bucks. It's like playing a competitive game in practice mode before you jump into ranked matches.

You get to make all the mistakes, test all the strategies, feel all the emotions of trading - without losing a single real dollar.

Why Paper Trading Is Genius

Think about how you learned to play your favorite game. Did you jump straight into ranked mode on day one? Probably not. You played tutorials. You practiced in creative mode. You watched YouTube videos. You experimented. You failed, learned, and tried again.

Paper trading lets you do exactly that for the stock market.

Here's what you can do in paper trading mode:

Buy and sell stocks with virtual money, using the exact same prices that real traders on Wall Street see.

Track your portfolio and see how your picks perform over days, weeks, and months.

Test strategies - try different approaches, different types of companies, different timing - all completely risk-free.

Build confidence so that when you're old enough and ready to invest real money, you already know exactly what you're doing with your money.

Platforms like **Thinkorswim paperMoney (by Charles Schwab)**, **Webull paper trading**, **TradingView**, and the **Investopedia Stock Simulator** all let you paper trade U.S. stocks for free. We'll walk through exactly how to set them up in Chapter 3. For now, just know that the tools exist and they're waiting for you.

Many of the best traders in the world still paper trade when they're testing new strategies. It's not a "kid thing" or a "beginner thing." It's a smart thing.

Gamer Tip: Paper trading is like creative mode in Minecraft. You have unlimited resources and zero consequences. Use this freedom to experiment wildly, make bold moves, and learn from every outcome. That's what practice is for. Take advantage of it.

A Real Example: Marcus's Paper Trading Journey

Let me tell you about Marcus. He's 14, lives in Austin, Texas, and loves playing Fortnite and chess online. One day during dinner, his mom mentioned that Tesla stock had jumped after a big earnings report. Marcus didn't know what an "earnings report" was, but he was curious. He Googled "how to trade stocks as a kid" and found Investopedia's Stock Simulator.

He started with $100,000 of virtual money (sounds like a fortune, but remember, it's all pretend). His first move was buying shares of Tesla because he thought the Cybertruck looked awesome. Then he bought some Apple stock because literally everyone at school had an iPhone. And he grabbed a few shares of Nike because he'd just bought a new pair of Air Jordans.

Within two weeks, his Tesla shares were up 6%, but his Nike pick had dropped 4% after news broke that a shipping delay would hurt their next quarter. He felt the sting of that loss - even though it wasn't real money. That emotional experience taught him something no textbook ever could: Remember, the market operates according to its own rules, not your emotions.

Over three months of paper trading, Marcus learned to read basic stock charts, set stop-losses (we'll cover these later), and manage his emotions when a trade went against him. He figured out that he was great at picking tech companies but terrible at timing when to sell. By the time he finished his first paper trading challenge, he understood more about money and risk than most adults he knew.

And he did it all without spending a single real dollar.

Setting Up Your Player Profile: What Kind of Trader Are You?

Before you jump into any game, you create your character. You pick your class, set your attributes, and decide how you want to play. Trading is no different.

Before we move forward in this book, I want you to think about three things. You don't need perfect answers right now - they'll evolve as you learn. But starting with intention matters.

1. Your Mindset

The stock market is not a get-rich-quick scheme. Anyone who tells you otherwise is either lying or trying to sell you something. The market is a skill-based game where patience, discipline, and continuous learning win over time.

Ask yourself: *Am I willing to treat this like learning a new game - starting from the basics, practicing regularly, and being patient with myself when I make mistakes?*

If your answer is yes, you're already ahead of 90% of people who try trading and give up because they expected instant results. It takes time to build a skill. So does this. Be Warned!

2. Your Goals

Every good gamer has goals. Maybe you want to hit a certain rank, unlock a specific achievement, or master a particular strategy. Your trading goals should be similar.

For now, your goal is simple: **become a confident, skilled paper trader who understands how the U.S. stock market works.** That's what this book will help you do. Not picking the hottest stock tip. Not getting rich overnight. Just building real, lasting knowledge and skill.

Later in the series, we'll set more specific goals. For Chapter 1, just commit to the journey.

3. Your Player Type

In games, there are different play styles. Some people are aggressive rushers, some are patient strategists, and some are careful builders. Trading has similar styles, and you'll discover yours as we go.

For now, think about how you play games:

The Careful Builder - You plan everything before you act. You read guides, study the map, and only make a move when you're sure. In trading, you might become a long-term investor who picks solid companies like Apple or Johnson & Johnson and holds them patiently for years.

The Strategic Raider - You like planned attacks with clear entry and exit strategies. You're calculated, not reckless. In trading, you might lean towards swing trading - holding stocks for a few days to a few weeks, riding momentum before taking profits.

The Speed Runner - You love fast action and quick decisions. You thrive on intensity. In trading, you might be drawn to day trading - buying and selling within the same day. But be warned: the U.S. has a Pattern Day Trader rule that requires $25,000 in your account to day trade freely, and speed without skill is just chaos.

There's no "best" type. Each have their own strengths and weaknesses. The important thing is to know your tendencies so you can build a trading approach that fits your personality.

Level 1 Complete - Your First XP Earned

Look at that. You've already cleared the first level.

Let's lock in what you've learned:

The stock market is a massive multiplayer game where companies are characters and stocks are your way of sharing in their growth. In the U.S., the two main arenas are the NYSE and NASDAQ, with the Dow Jones and S&P 500 as the top leaderboards.

Starting young is your cheat code. Compound interest rewards early players with exponential growth over time. Warren Buffett bought his first stock at 11. Every year you start earlier is worth more than you can imagine.

Paper trading is your practice server. It gives you all the learning with zero financial risk. Platforms like Thinkorswim, Webull, and Investopedia's Simulator let you trade with virtual cash using real market prices. Every professional trader uses practice trading - there's no shame in it, only smart strategy. Practice makes you better!

Know your player type. Your mindset, goals, and natural play style will shape how you trade. There's no single right way - only the way that fits you.

Chapter 1 Mission

Before you move to Chapter 2, complete this quick mission. You have two paths to choose from. Pick the one that fits your style-or use both.

Path A: The Journal

Step 1: Open a notebook or a note on your phone. Write "My Paper Trading Journal" at the top. This is the beginning of your trade journal, and you'll use it throughout this entire book.

Step 2: Write down your answers to these three questions: What excites me most about learning the stock market? What kind of gamer am I - Careful Builder, Strategic Raider, or Speed Runner? What's one company I use every day that I'd like to learn more about as a stock?

Step 3: Look up the S&P 500 index on Google. Just search "S&P 500 today." See the number? That's the current score of America's top 500 companies. Write it down in your journal with today's date. We'll check back on this number later.

Mission time: 10 minutes. Difficulty: Easy. XP earned: Your first step into the arena.

Path B: The Mission Log Dashboard

You can track everything digitally-and earn XP while doing it-open the Paper Trading Boss Battles Mission Log Dashboard. Create your account on the website – HTTPS://WWW.PTBOSSBATTLES.COM It's the interactive companion built for this book series. Navigate to Chapter 1 and complete these three missions:

Player Profile (+100 XP)-Enter your trader name, pick your avatar, and fill in your starting details. This is your character creation screen.

Risk Class Quiz (+150 XP)-Answer six scenario-based questions and discover whether you're a Guardian Tank, an All-Rounder, or an Attacker. The dashboard scores it automatically and shows your strengths and weaknesses.

My Trading Why (+100 XP)-Write down why you trade, what inspires you, and what your dream is. This is your anchor. When things get hard later in the book, you'll come back here.

Still look up the S&P 500 today and note the number. Whether you wrote it in a notebook or typed it into the dashboard, that number is your starting line.

~ ~ ~

Both paths accomplish the same thing: you define who you are as a trader before you ever place a trade. The journal keeps it personal and portable. The dashboard keeps it structured and tracks your XP across every chapter of every book. Either way, you just built your loadout.

Coming Up Next: Learning the Controls

You've chosen to enter the arena. You've created your player profile. You know what the stock market is, why it matters, and how paper trading lets you jump in without risk.

But every game has controls you need to master before you can actually play. Imagine jumping into Fortnite without knowing how to build, or starting a chess game without knowing how the pieces move. You'd be lost in seconds.

The stock market has its own vocabulary - its own set of controls. Words like *portfolio, dividends, bull market, bear market, market cap* they sound complicated, but once you decode them, they're as natural as knowing what "respawn" or "loot" means in a game.

In Chapter 2, we'll decode every essential term you need to know. We'll turn confusing Wall Street jargon into a language you can speak fluently. Consider it your HUD setup - the heads-up display that shows you everything happening in the game.

The controls are waiting. Let's learn them.

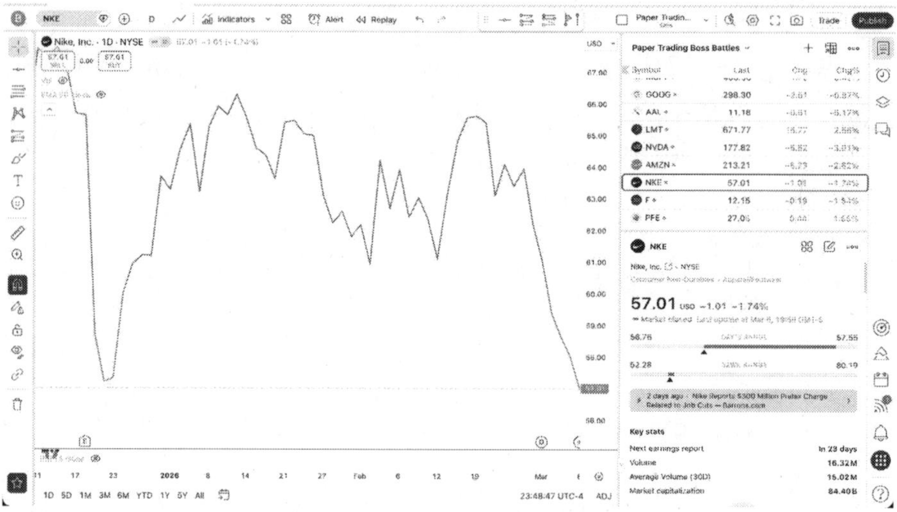

Trading HUD

Chapter 2

Learning the Controls - Stock Market Vocabulary Decoded

CONGRATS ON TAKING UP THE PLAYER MODE IN STOCK MARKET.

Every game has controls you need to master before you can play.

Imagine jumping into Fortnite without knowing how to build. You land, grab a weapon, the storm is closing in - and some player throws up a three-story tower in two seconds while you're still trying to figure out which button places a wall. You'd get eliminated before you understood what happened.

The stock market has its own controls, too. They're not buttons on a controller - they're words. Terms. Vocabulary. And if you don't understand them, every headline, every chart, and every conversation about money will feel like a foreign language.

But here's the good news: there aren't that many words to learn. And once you know them, they click into place fast - like finally memorizing your keybinds and suddenly the game feels smooth and natural.

In this chapter, we're decoding the essential stock market vocabulary. By the end, you'll be able to read a financial headline from CNBC or Bloomberg and actually understand it. Think of this as setting up your HUD - the heads-up display that shows you everything happening in the game.

Let's get your controls mapped.

Stocks, Shares, and Equity - Owning a Piece of the Game

Let's start with the three words you'll hear more than any others: **stock**, **share**, and **equity**. People use them almost interchangeably, and that can get confusing. So let's break them down.

A **stock** represents ownership in a company. When a company like Tesla decides it wants to raise money from the public, it divides itself into millions of tiny, equal pieces. Each of those pieces is called a **share**. When you buy a share of Tesla, you literally own a tiny fraction of the company - its stores, its cars, its cash in the bank, all of it.

Think of it like this. You and three friends build an incredible Minecraft world together and agree to own it equally - 25% each. Those are your "shares." If the world gets famous and a fifth person wants in, they'd need to buy shares from one of you. The price depends on how awesome the world is.

Equity is just a fancier word for ownership. When someone says "I have equity in a company," they mean they own some of it. Stock, share, equity - they're all circling around the same idea: you own a piece of something.

Gamer Translation: Stock = the game. Share = one copy of the game in your inventory. Equity = proof that the copy belongs to you. You're not just a player anymore - you're a part-owner of the studio! Isn't that cool?

Why Do Companies Sell Shares?

Companies sell shares for the same reason a Roblox developer sells in-game passes - to raise money so they can grow. When a company sells shares to the public for the very first time, it's called an **IPO (Initial Public Offering)**. Think of it as the game's launch day. Before the IPO, only founders and early investors owned pieces. After, anyone with a brokerage account can buy shares.

When Rivian, the electric truck company, had its IPO in November 2021, investors went wild. The stock shot up on day one and briefly made Rivian worth more than Ford - a company that had been making cars for over a hundred years. That's the power of an IPO. Everyone wants in on the new release, just like gamers lining up for a midnight drop.

Your Inventory and Your Loot - Portfolios, Dividends, and Market Cap

Now that you know what stocks and shares are, let's talk about how you organize them and how they reward you.

Portfolio: Your Inventory

In every game, you have an inventory - a place where all your weapons, items, and resources are stored. In trading, your inventory is called your **portfolio**.

Your portfolio is simply the collection of all the stocks (and other investments) you own. If you buy shares in Apple, Tesla, and Coca-Cola, those three stocks make up your portfolio. A good portfolio is like a well-balanced game loadout - you don't want to put everything into one slot.

A portfolio with only tech stocks is like going into a battle with five snipers and no medic. If tech has a bad day, everything suffers. But if you spread your stocks across different types of companies - tech, healthcare, food, banks - one bad sector won't wipe you out. This idea of spreading your bets is called **diversification**, and it's one of the most important concepts in investing.

Dividends: Passive Loot

Some games reward you just for logging in. You open the app, and there's a daily chest with gold or gems waiting for you. You didn't do anything - the game just handed you free loot.

Dividends work the same way. Some companies take a portion of their profits and send cash directly to their shareholders on a regular schedule - usually every three months (quarterly). You own the stock, and the company pays you just for holding it. It's passive loot.

Not every company pays dividends. Fast-growing tech companies like Amazon and Tesla usually don't - they prefer to reinvest every dollar back into the business. But older, established companies like Coca-Cola,

Johnson & Johnson, and Procter & Gamble are famous for paying steady dividends year after year. Coca-Cola has paid a dividend for over 60 years straight. That's a daily login reward running since the 1960s.

Gamer Translation: Dividends = daily login rewards. You don't have to do anything extra. Just hold the stock, and the company drops cash into your account every few months.

Market Capitalization: A Company's Power Level

In Dragon Ball Z, characters have power levels. In the stock market, companies have something similar called **market capitalization** (or **market cap** for short).

Market cap is calculated by multiplying a company's stock price by the total number of shares that exist. It tells you the total value the market places on the entire company.

Here's an example. If Microsoft's stock price is $400 and there are about 7.3 billion shares, Microsoft's market cap is roughly $3 trillion. That makes Microsoft one of the most valuable companies on Earth.

Companies are grouped by their power level:

Large-cap ($10 billion and above): The titans. Apple, Microsoft, Amazon, Google, JPMorgan Chase. These are the endgame bosses of the stock market - massive, powerful, and hard to take down. They're considered the safest bets for beginners.

Mid-cap ($2 billion to $10 billion): Strong players that are still growing. They've proven themselves but haven't reached max level yet. Companies like Etsy or Five Below fit here.

Small-cap (under $2 billion): Newer or smaller companies with higher risk but also higher potential reward. They're the up-and-coming characters that could become legends - or get eliminated early.

For your paper trading journey, we'll focus mostly on large-cap U.S . stocks. They're the best training ground because they're well-known, heavily traded, and easier to research.

Attack Mode vs. Defense Mode - Bulls, Bears, and How Prices Move

If you watch even five minutes of financial news, you'll hear two animal names tossed around constantly: **bulls** and **bears**. They sound random, but they're the most important mood indicators in the entire market.

Bull Market: Attack Mode

A **bull market** is when stock prices are rising and investors feel optimistic. The economy is growing, companies are making money, and people keep buying because they believe prices will keep climbing.

Think of it as Attack Mode. Everyone's pushing forward, landing hits, racking up points. The vibe is pure confidence. The name comes from how a bull attacks - it thrusts its horns upward. Bull = up.

The U.S. experienced one of the longest bull markets in history from 2009 to 2020 - over a decade of prices mostly going up. If you had invested $1,000 in the S&P 500 at the start of that bull run, it would have grown to roughly $5,000 by the end. That's the power of Attack Mode in the market.

Bear Market: Defense Mode

A **bear market** is the opposite. Prices are falling, the economy looks shaky, and investors get nervous. People sell stocks because they're afraid prices will drop further.

This is Defense Mode. Everyone's retreating, building walls, protecting what they have. The name comes from how a bear swipes its paws downward. Bear = down.

Officially, a bear market is defined as a drop of 20% or more from recent highs. The U.S. hit a bear market in early 2020 when COVID-19 shut down the economy. The S&P 500 fell over 30% in just weeks. People panicked. But here's the twist - the market recovered within months and hit new all-time highs. Players who stayed calm during Defense Mode and didn't panic-sell were rewarded massively.

Gamer Translation: Bull market = the whole server is in Attack Mode, pushing aggressively. Bear market = everyone's in Defense Mode, building walls and playing safe. Great traders know how to play both.

Supply and Demand: The Roblox Limited-Item Auction

So what actually makes stock prices go up or down on any given day? The answer is the most fundamental rule in economics: **supply and demand**.

If you've ever played Roblox, you know how limited-edition items work. When Roblox releases a limited hat, the supply is fixed - only a certain number exist. If tons of players want it, but only a few copies are available, the price skyrockets. Now flip it. If that hat falls out of fashion and nobody wants it, sellers keep dropping their price just to find a buyer. Price crashes.

Stocks work on the exact same principle. Every second during market hours, buyers and sellers are negotiating. The stock price you see at any moment is simply the last price someone agreed to pay.

When more people want to buy than sell (high demand), the price goes up . When more people want to sell than buy (high supply), the price goes down . It's a never-ending auction - millions of transactions, all day, every trading day. That's not random chaos - it's millions of players making decisions based on their beliefs, information, and emotions.

Reading the Scoreboard - Understanding the Dow Jones and S&P 500

We mentioned the Dow Jones and S&P 500 briefly in Chapter 1. Now let's really understand them, because these two leaderboards will be your constant companions on this trading journey.

The Dow Jones Industrial Average (DJIA)

The **Dow Jones Industrial Average** - usually just called "the Dow" - is a list of 30 massive, blue-chip American companies. "Blue-chip" is a term borrowed from poker, where the blue chips are worth the most. So blue-chip companies are the heavyweights - companies like Apple, Microsoft, Walt Disney, Goldman Sachs, Visa, and Nike.

The Dow has been around since 1896 - it's the oldest major stock index in the U.S. When the evening news says "The market was up 300 points today," they're almost always talking about the Dow.

But here's a secret that even a lot of adults don't know: the Dow only tracks 30 companies out of thousands. It's like judging an entire Fortnite tournament based only on the top 30 players - you get a general idea, but you miss a lot.

The S&P 500

That's where the **S&P 500** comes in. It tracks 500 of the largest publicly traded companies in the United States, covering about 80% of the total value of the American stock market. That makes it a much more complete picture than the Dow.

If the Dow is the Top 30 ranked players, the S&P 500 is the entire competitive tier list. It includes tech giants like Apple and NVIDIA, healthcare companies like UnitedHealth, banks like JPMorgan Chase, retailers like Amazon, and energy companies like ExxonMobil.

Most professional investors and fund managers measure their performance against the S&P 500. When someone says "I beat the market this year," they usually mean they made more money than the S&P 500 did. It's the benchmark - the final score everyone compares themselves to.

Reading a Real Headline

Let's put your new vocabulary to work with a real headline you might see on CNBC:

"S&P 500 rises 1.2% as tech stocks rally; Apple and NVIDIA lead gains amid strong earnings reports."

Before this chapter, that sentence might have looked like a foreign language. Now you can decode every piece:

S&P 500 rises 1.2% - The top 500 U.S. companies collectively went up 1.2% today. Bull mode.

Tech stocks rally - Technology stocks had a particularly strong day. A "rally" means prices jumped up quickly.

Apple and NVIDIA lead gains - Among all the stocks that rose, Apple and NVIDIA rose the most.

Strong earnings reports - These companies reported quarterly profits better than expected, boosting confidence and driving buyers in.

See? You just read a real Wall Street headline like a pro. That's what happens when you learn the controls.

Case Study: Zoe's First Week Reading the Market

Zoe is 15 and lives in Denver, Colorado. After reading Chapter 1, she decided to start paying attention to the stock market. She didn't trade anything yet - she just started watching.

On Monday, she searched "S&P 500 today" on Google and saw it was up 0.8%. She read that Amazon had reported strong earnings. She thought, "Amazon's quarterly results were good, investors are buying shares, and that's pushing the S&P 500 up. Supply and demand in action."

On Wednesday, the market dropped 1.5%. She panicked for a second, but then read that the Federal Reserve had hinted at raising interest rates. She didn't fully understand interest rates yet (we'll get there), but she recognized the pattern: bad news from a major authority made investors nervous, so they sold stocks. More sellers than buyers. Prices fell. Defense Mode.

On Friday, she noticed that her favorite brand, Nike, had dropped 3% after announcing that supply chain issues would delay new sneaker releases. She connected the dots: negative company news led to lower earnings expectations, which caused investors to sell Nike shares. The stock's "power level" took a temporary hit.

By the end of one week, Zoe could read financial headlines, spot bull and bear vibes, and understand the mechanics behind price changes. She hadn't spent a dollar. She'd just learned the controls.

Your Vocabulary Cheat Sheet

Here's every key term from this chapter in one place. Screenshot it or bookmark this page - you'll use these words for the rest of the series.

Stock / Share / Equity: All mean ownership. A stock is ownership in a company. A share is one unit of that stock. Equity is another word for the same idea.

IPO (Initial Public Offering): The first time a company sells its shares to the public. Launch day for a stock.

Portfolio: Your collection of all the stocks and investments you own. Your inventory.

Diversification: Spreading your money across different stocks and sectors so one bad pick doesn't wreck everything.

Dividends: Cash payments companies send to shareholders from their profits. Passive loot.

Market Cap: Total value of a company (stock price × total shares). Large-cap = titans ($10B+). Mid-cap = strong contenders ($2–10B). Small-cap = up-and-comers (under $2B).

Bull Market: A market where prices are rising and the vibe is optimistic. Attack Mode.

Bear Market: A market where prices are falling (20%+ from highs) and the vibe is cautious. Defense Mode.

Supply and Demand: The force that moves prices. More buyers than sellers = price goes up. More sellers than buyers = price goes down.

Dow Jones (the Dow): Leaderboard tracking 30 of the biggest U.S. companies. **S&P 500:** Leaderboard tracking 500 of the largest - the benchmark most pros use.

Earnings Report: A company's quarterly "report card" showing how much money it made. Strong earnings = stock often goes up. Weak earnings = stock often goes down.

Level 2 Complete - Controls Mapped

You just installed the HUD. Every piece of information you see on a stock screen or a financial news feed now has a label you recognize.

Let's lock in the key takeaways:

Stocks, shares, and equity all mean ownership. When you buy a share, you own a tiny piece of a real company. An IPO is when a company first goes public and lets anyone buy in.

Your portfolio is your inventory. Diversify it across different types of companies so you're not wiped out by one bad pick. Dividends are passive loot - some companies pay you just for owning their stock. Market cap tells you a company's power level.

Bull markets and bear markets are the two modes of the game. Prices move based on supply and demand - like the same force that makes limited Roblox items spike in price.

The Dow Jones and S&P 500 are your scoreboards. The Dow tracks 30 heavyweights. The S&P 500 tracks 500 top companies and gives you the most complete picture of the U.S. market.

Chapter 2 Mission

Before you move to Chapter 3, complete this mission to lock in your XP. Pick your path:

Path A: The Journal

Step 1: Open your Paper Trading Journal from Chapter 1. On a new page, write "My Vocabulary Log." Copy down the five terms from this chapter that were newest to you. Write each one in your own words - pretend you're explaining them to a friend who's never heard of the stock market.

Step 2: Search Google for "CNBC markets today" or "Bloomberg markets." Read one headline from the front page. Try to decode it using the terms you learned in this chapter. Write down the headline and your translation in your journal.

Step 3: Pick three companies you use in real life - maybe Apple, Nike, and Disney. Search each one followed by "stock" on Google. Write down the stock price and market cap for each. Which one has the highest power level?

Mission time: 15 minutes. Difficulty: Easy. XP earned: You can now read the market's HUD.

Path B: The Mission Log Dashboard

If you'd rather level up digitally, open the Paper Trading Boss Battles Mission Log Dashboard. Navigate to Chapter 4: Beginner Missions and launch the Vocabulary Quest. Here's what's waiting for you:

Vocabulary Quest (+200 XP)-Twenty trading terms are split into six categories: Basics, Trends, Charts, Trading, Indices, and Risk. You click a term on the left, then click its matching definition on the right. It's a matching game, and the dashboard tracks your score in real time. Match fifteen or more to complete the mission.

Fill-in-the-Blank Challenge -Below the matching game, five sentences are missing a key term. Fill in the blanks to prove you didn't just memorize-you actually understand. Questions like "The ___ is the largest stock exchange" and "A ___ order auto-sells at a set level" test whether the vocabulary stuck.

Even if you use the dashboard, still do the real-world piece: look up three companies you use every day, check their stock price and market cap, and figure out which one has the highest power level. The dashboard teaches you the terms. The real world shows you where they live.

~ ~ ~

Both paths prove the same thing: you can read the market's heads-up display now. The journal makes you write the definitions from memory. The dashboard quizzes you with an interactive matching game and fill-in-the-blank challenges. One is analog, one is digital-both lock the language into your brain.

Coming Up Next: Choosing Your Server

You know the language now. You can decode headlines, understand what a stock is, identify bull and bear markets, and read the major scoreboards. Your controls are mapped and your HUD is live.

But knowing the controls isn't the same as playing the game. You need a place to actually play.

In Chapter 3, we're setting you up with a real paper trading platform. We'll walk through the best free tools for U.S. stock market paper trading - Thinkorswim paperMoney, Webull, TradingView, and Investopedia's

Stock Simulator. You'll create your account, learn the interface, and place your very first simulated trade.

You wouldn't play Minecraft on a laggy server with no mods. Picking the right paper trading platform matters just as much. Let's choose your server. Charge On!

Chapter 3

Choosing Your Server - Where and How to Paper Trade

You wouldn't play Minecraft on a laggy server with no mods.

Seriously. If you're about to spend hours building, exploring, and battling, you want a server that runs smooth, loads fast, and gives you the tools you need. A bad server ruins the whole experience. A great server makes you never want to log off.

Picking the right paper trading platform works the same way. The platform is where you'll spend your time analyzing stocks, placing trades, and tracking your results. Choose a clunky one, and you'll get frustrated before you even learn anything. Choose the right one, and the whole experience clicks into place.

In this chapter, we're going to explore the best free paper trading platforms available for U.S. stocks. We'll walk through how to set up your first account, understand the trading interface, learn the different types of orders you can place, and - best of all - you'll place your very first paper trade before this chapter ends.

Time to choose your server.

The Four Best Paper Trading Platforms for Beginners

There are dozens of paper trading tools out there, but not all of them are built for beginners. Some are designed for professionals with twenty years of experience. Others look like they haven't been updated since 2005. You need a platform that's free, easy to navigate, uses real U.S. market data, and doesn't make you feel like you need a finance degree just to find the "Buy" button.

Here are the four platforms I recommend. Each one has a different personality, just like game servers.

1. Investopedia Stock Simulator

If paper trading platforms were game difficulty settings, Investopedia's Stock Simulator would be **Easy Mode**. It's the most beginner-friendly platform on this list, and it's completely free.

You start with $100,000 of virtual cash. The interface is clean and simple - To buy a stock, just search for it, click "Buy," pick the number of shares you want, and you're all set!. There are no confusing menus, no overwhelming charts, and no advanced tools cluttering the screen. It's designed for people who are learning, not people who already know everything.

Investopedia also has an incredible library of articles and tutorials built right into the site, so if you don't understand a term, the explanation is one click away. Think of it as a server with a built-in tutorial area.

Best for: Absolute beginners who want a clean, simple experience with zero overwhelm.

2. TradingView Paper Trading

TradingView is like the **Creative Mode** of trading platforms, offering some of the most powerful charting tools out there-all for free! Professional traders from all over the globe use TradingView for their charts, and the paper trading feature lets you practice trades right on those charts.

The interface might seem a bit more complex than Investopedia, as you're seeing real stock charts with price candles, volume bars, and indicators. But that's actually a great thing. You'll naturally start learning to read charts while you trade, which is a skill you'll need in Chapters 6 through 8.

TradingView also has a huge community. You can follow other traders, see their chart ideas, and learn from how they analyze stocks. It's like joining a Minecraft server where the best builders show off their techniques. I wonder if they thought in terms of Minecraft whey they built it.

Best for: Beginners who want to learn chart reading alongside paper trading. This is the platform we'll use most in this book series.

3. Webull Paper Trading

Webull is a real brokerage app that also offers a built-in paper trading mode. It feels like playing on a **Ranked Practice Server** - the interface is the same one real traders use, but your money is virtual.

The Webull app is sleek and modern, works great on your phone, and gives you access to real-time U.S. stock data, financial news, and even a community feed where traders discuss their picks. The paper trading mode starts you with $1,000,000 of virtual cash.

The advantage of Webull is that when you're eventually ready to move from paper trading to real trading (years from now), you won't need to learn a new platform. You'll already know exactly how the interface works.

Best for: Teens who want a mobile-first experience and like the idea of practising on a real brokerage app.

4. Thinkorswim paperMoney (by Charles Schwab)

Thinkorswim is the **Expert Dungeon** of trading platforms. It's the most advanced tool on this list, packed with professional-grade features: advanced charting, options chains, technical studies, scanners, and more tools than you'll know what to do with right now.

The paperMoney feature gives you $100,000 of virtual cash to trade stocks, ETFs, and even options using the same interface that professional traders on Wall Street use. The learning curve is steeper, but the payoff is huge. If you master Thinkorswim, you can handle any platform.

Best for: Ambitious beginners who don't mind a challenge and want to grow into a professional-level platform. Great to explore later in your journey.

Author's Tip: Start with Investopedia or TradingView. Get comfortable. Then try Webull or Thinkorswim when you're ready for a harder server. No need to hurry-the best players take their time, leveling up one server at a time.

Part 1

Setting Up Your First Paper Trading Account

Let's get you into the game. After giving it some thought, I've decided to proceed in the same way I showed my younger friends. We'll walk through setting up an account on **TradingView**, since it's the platform we'll reference most throughout this book series. The process is quick, free, and doesn't require any real money or parental brokerage accounts. Please let your parents know what you're up to here, so they know this is your trading practice server.

Step-by-Step: Getting Started on TradingView

Step 1: Go to TradingView website - To get started with TradingView, simply open your browser and type in this referral link:

https://tinyurl.com/bdejk6rk

You can also download the TradingView app on your phone or tablet. By using the above link, you'll receive a $15 credit towards any paid plans once you complete the Paper Trading Boss Battles series and become a pro trader. However, for this book, we'll be using the free version of TradingView.

Step 2: Create a free account. Click "Sign Up" in the top right corner. You can sign up with an email address or link it to your Google account. The free plan gives you everything you need as a beginner.

Step 3: Search for a stock. Once you're logged in, you'll see a search bar at the top. Type in a stock symbol - try "AAPL" for Apple. A chart will pop up showing Apple's price history. Don't worry about reading the chart yet. We'll get there in Chapter 6.

Step 4: Open the Paper Trading panel. At the top right of the chart screen, look for a 'Trade' button and click it, then select "Paper Trading" and connect. You will now see a bottom panel for trading. TradingView will give you $100,000 of virtual cash to start. Your practice server is now live.

Step 5: Place your first paper trade. Click "Buy" on the trading panel, select how many shares you want (start small - try 10 shares of Apple), and confirm. That's it. You just bought your first stock.

The whole process takes about five minutes. You don't need a credit card, a bank account, or your parents' permission to set up a paper trading account. It's purely educational, and no real money is involved.

Gamer Tip: Your first paper trade doesn't need to be perfect. It doesn't even need to make money. The goal right now is just to feel what it's like to click "Buy" and watch a real stock move in your portfolio. That first click is your character's first step into the arena.

Part 2

Understanding the Trading Interface - Your Game Dashboard

When you first open a trading platform, it can look overwhelming. Charts, numbers, flashing colors, scrolling tickers - it's a lot. But just like a game dashboard, every piece of information has a purpose. Let's decode the main elements so you know exactly what you're looking at.

The Watchlist: Your Favorites List

A **watchlist** is a custom list of stocks you want to keep an eye on. It's like a favorites list or a bookmarked playlist. Instead of searching for Apple, Tesla, and Nike every single time you log in, you add them to your watchlist once and they're always right there.

Every platform has a watchlist feature. On TradingView, you'll find it on the right side of the screen. Click the "+" button, type a stock symbol, and it's added. Build a watchlist of five to ten stocks you're interested in - companies you use, brands you know, names you recognize

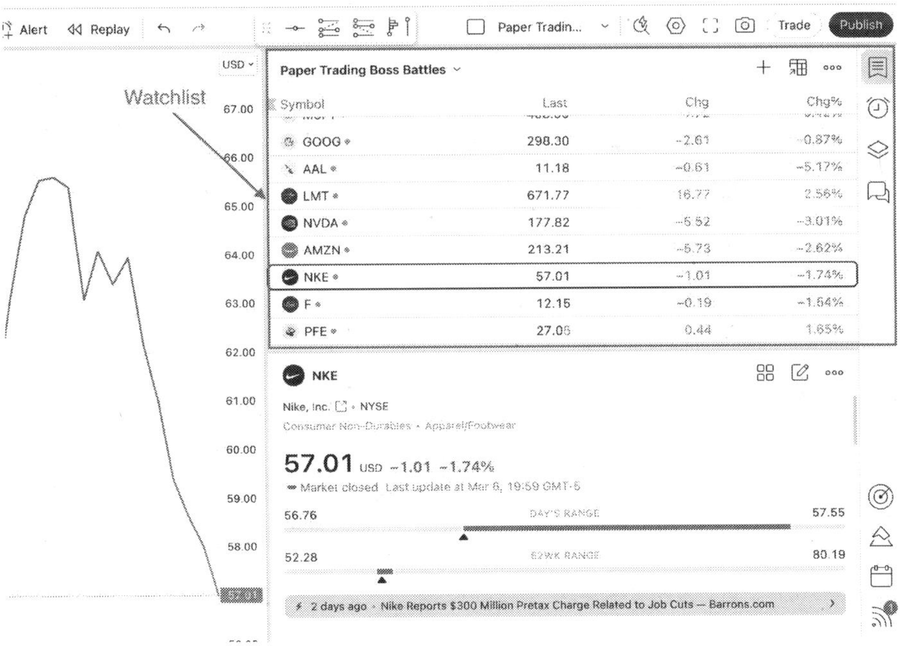

Watchlist

The Chart: Your Battle Map

The chart is the big visual display in the center of the screen. It shows a stock's price movement over time. Think of it as the battle map - it tells you where the stock has been and hints at where it might go.

For now, don't stress about reading every detail. Just notice the basics: the line or candles show price going up (green) or down (red), the time axis runs along the bottom, and the price axis runs along the right side. We'll dive deep into charts in Chapter 6.

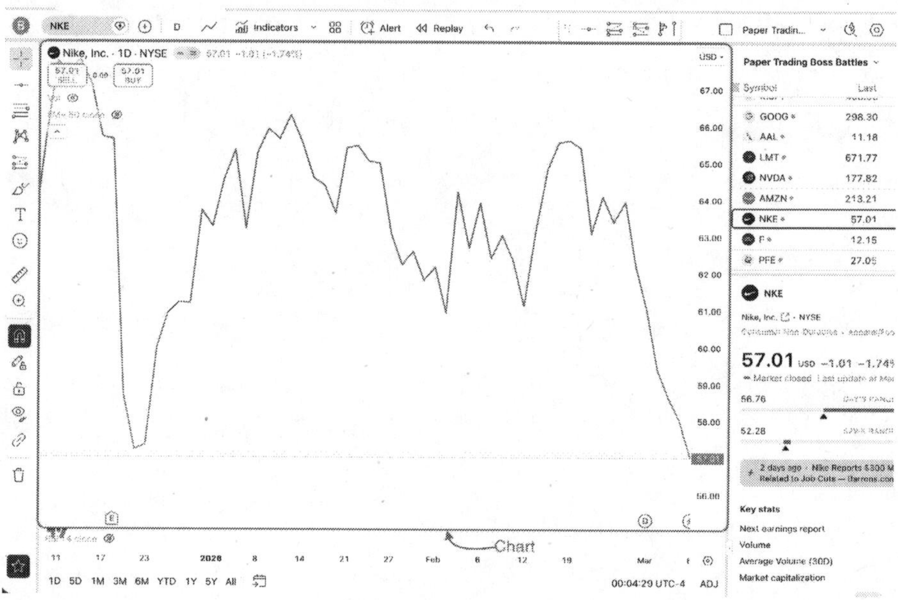

Chart

The Portfolio View: Your Inventory Screen

Once you place trades, you need a place to see everything you own. That's your **portfolio view** - the inventory screen of trading. It shows you every stock you've bought, how many shares you hold, what you paid, and whether you're currently up or down on each position.

The portfolio view also shows your total account value. You started with $100,000 of virtual cash. After a few trades, that number will change based on how your picks are performing. Green means your portfolio is up. Red means it's down. Over time, you want to see that total number growing.

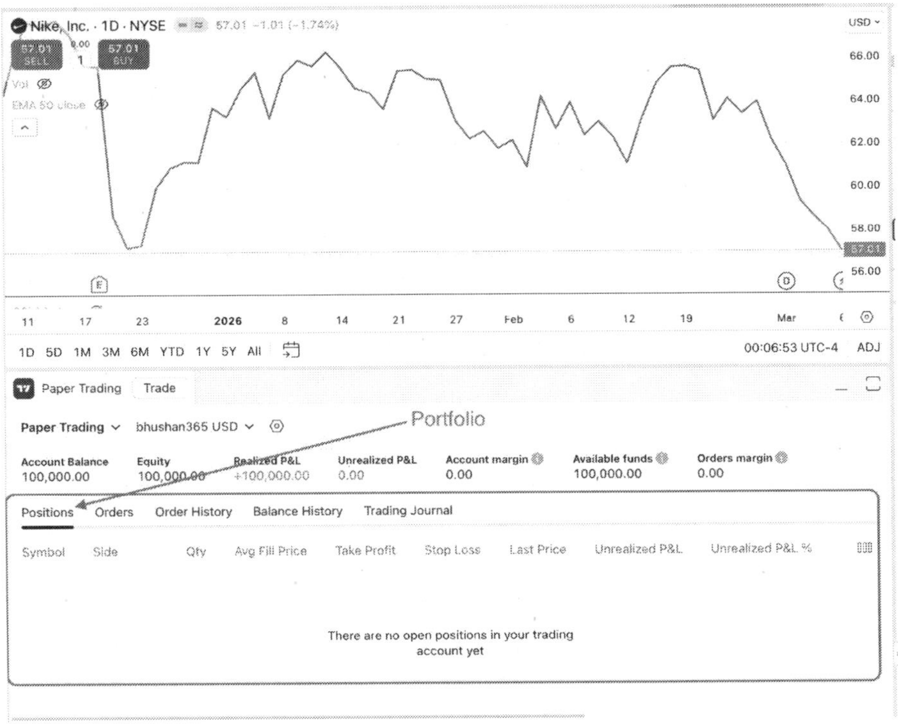

Portfolio

The Order Book: The Trading Counter

The **order book** shows you all the current buy and sell orders for a stock. It's like looking at the auction house in a game - you can see what prices buyers are offering and what prices sellers are asking.

As a beginner, you won't need to obsess over the order book. But it's good to know it exists. It's the raw engine of supply and demand you learned about in Chapter 2, happening in real time.

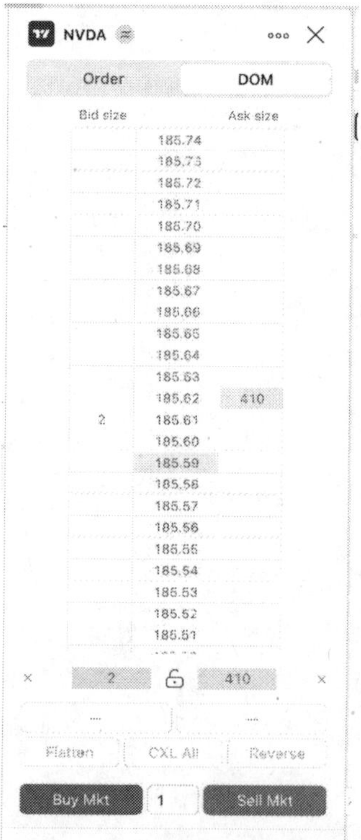

Order Book Showing 410 shares asking to sell @ $185.62 and 2 ready to buy @185.61

Types of Orders - How to Actually Buy and Sell

In most games, buying something is simple. You walk up to a shop, click the item, and pay. Stock trading has a few more options because *how* you buy matters just as much as *what* you buy. Let's learn the three order types every paper trader needs to know.

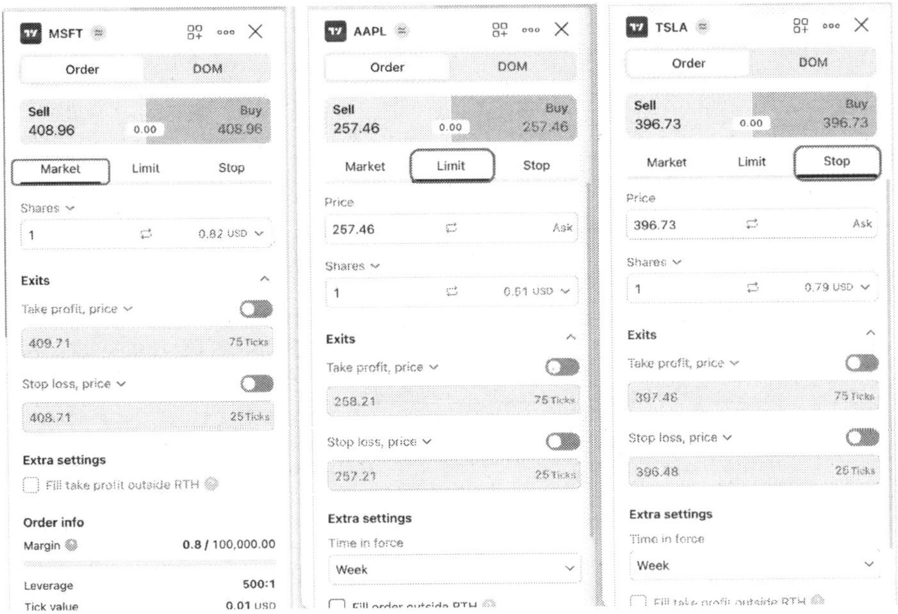

Types of Orders

Market Order: The Instant Buy

A **market order** is the simplest trade you can make. You're saying: "I want to buy (or sell) this stock right now, at whatever the current price is."

It's like walking into a store and buying something at the price on the tag. No negotiation, no waiting. You click "Buy," and the trade happens almost instantly during market hours.

Market orders are great when you want speed. The downside? If a stock's price is jumping around quickly, you might pay slightly more (or sell for slightly less) than the price you saw when you clicked.

When to use it: When you want to get into a trade quickly and the stock's price isn't moving wildly.

Limit Order: Setting a Trap

A **limit order** lets you name your price. Instead of buying at whatever the stock costs right now, you tell the platform: "I only want to buy if the price drops to $X."

Think of it like setting a trap in a game. You place it at a specific location and wait. If the target walks into the trap, it triggers. If not, nothing happens.

Here's an example. Apple is currently trading at $250. You think it's a good buy, but you'd rather get it at $245. You set a limit order to buy at $245. If Apple's price drops to $245 at any point, your order automatically executes. If it never drops that low, the order just sits there waiting.

When to use it: When you have a specific price in mind and you're willing to wait for it. Patient players love limit orders.

Stop-Loss Order: Your Auto-Shield

This is the most important order type for protecting yourself. A **stop-loss order** automatically sells your stock if the price falls to a certain level. It's your emergency exit - your auto-shield that activates when things go wrong.

Say you buy Tesla at $400. You decide you're okay with losing a little, but you don't want to lose more than $25 per share. You set a stop-loss at

$375. If Tesla drops to $375, the platform automatically sells your shares, limiting your loss.

Without a stop-loss, a small loss can turn into a massive loss while you're at school, sleeping, or just not paying attention. A stop-loss is like an insurance policy. It doesn't prevent bad things from happening, but it controls the damage.

When to use it: Always. Every single trade. We'll hammer this point throughout the entire series. Professional traders never enter a position without knowing their exit.

Gamer Translation:

Market order = instant buy from the shop.

Limit order = setting a trap at a specific price.

Stop-loss = an auto-shield that ejects you before you take too much damage.

Learn all three. Use all three.

Case Study: Ethan's First Trading Session

Ethan is 16, lives in Chicago, and decided to start paper trading after reading the first two chapters. Here's exactly how his first session went.

He opened TradingView on his laptop after school, created a free account in about three minutes, and activated the Paper Trading panel. He started with $100,000 of virtual cash.

First, he built a watchlist. He added five stocks he knew: Apple (AAPL), Microsoft (MSFT), Nike (NKE), Coca-Cola (KO), and Amazon (AMZN). He picked companies he used in real life, just like we suggested in Chapter 1.

Then he placed his first trade. He bought 20 shares of Apple at $250 using a **market order**. It cost him $5,000 of his virtual cash. He watched the price tick up a few cents and felt a little jolt of excitement - even though it wasn't real money.

Next, he set a **limit order** to buy 15 shares of Nike at $50. Nike was currently trading at $57, so the order didn't execute right away. It just sat there, waiting for the price to drop. He liked the idea of being patient and letting the trap do the work.

Finally, he went back to his Apple trade and set a **stop-loss at $240**. That meant if Apple dropped $10 from his buy price, his shares would automatically sell. He decided he was comfortable risking $10 per share but no more.

His entire first session took about 20 minutes. He didn't make any money. He didn't lose any money (yet). But he had a watchlist, an open position, a pending limit order, and a stop-loss in place. He was officially in the game.

Over the next few days, Ethan checked his portfolio during lunch. Apple had gone up slightly. His Nike limit order still hadn't triggered. He learned something important: trading isn't constant action. A lot of it is watching, waiting, and letting your plan play out. The patience felt familiar - it was exactly like waiting for the right moment to attack in chess.

Level 3 Complete - You're in the Game

You just chose your server and entered the arena. This is a big moment. Most people talk about wanting to learn about stocks. You've actually done something about it.

Let's lock in what you've learned:

Four platforms, four personalities. Investopedia is Easy Mode. TradingView is Creative Mode. Webull is Ranked Practice. Thinkorswim is the Expert Dungeon. Start simple, upgrade later.

Setting up takes five minutes. A free TradingView account gives you $100,000 of virtual cash, powerful charts, and a paper trading panel. No credit card, no bank account needed.

The interface has four key areas. The watchlist (favorites), the chart (battle map), the portfolio view (inventory), and the order book (auction house). You don't need to master all of them today. Just know where things are.

Three order types are essential. Market orders for instant buys, limit orders for patient traps, and stop-loss orders for protection. Use all three, especially stop-losses.

Chapter 3 Mission

This is your most important mission yet because it moves you from reading about trading to actually doing it. Pick your path:

Path A: The Journal

Step 1: Create a free account on TradingView (or Investopedia Stock Simulator if you prefer a simpler start). Activate the Paper Trading feature.

Step 2: Build a watchlist of five U.S. stocks. Pick companies you know and use. Here are some ideas to get started: Apple (AAPL), Amazon (AMZN), Nike (NKE), Coca-Cola (KO), Google (GOOGL), Disney (DIS), Tesla (TSLA), Microsoft (MSFT).

Step 3: Place your first paper trade. Buy at least 10 shares of one company using a market order. Don't overthink it - just pick one and click "Buy."

Step 4: Set a stop-loss on your trade. Decide the maximum you're willing to lose per share and set the stop-loss at that level.

Step 5: Record everything in your Paper Trading Journal. Write down what you bought, how many shares, at what price, where you set your stop-loss, and why you picked that company.

Mission time: 20 minutes. Difficulty: Medium. XP earned: You're now an active paper trader.

Path B: The Mission Log Dashboard

If you want structure and XP tracking, open the Paper Trading Boss Battles Mission Log Dashboard. Two missions across two chapters walk you through exactly what this chapter asks you to do:

Trading Setup Checklist (+150 XP)-Navigate to Chapter 4: Beginner Missions and open Trading Setup. It's a ten-step interactive checklist: create your TradingView account, build a watchlist, add SPY as your benchmark, configure your charts with daily candles and indicators, open paper trading, and place your first trade. Check off eight or more to complete it.

Log Trades (+250 XP)-Navigate to Chapter 2: Trade Log and open Log Trades. This is your digital trade journal. Log your first paper trade with the full breakdown: date, ticker, direction, entry price, exit price, shares, stop-loss, target, confluence signals, emotional state at entry and exit, whether you followed your plan, and a one-sentence lesson. Every field the journal asks for, the dashboard captures in structured form.

Before you log that first trade, take a look at the Sample Trade mission in the same chapter. It shows a pre-filled NVDA trade with annotations explaining what goes in every field and why. Think of it as the tutorial level before you play for real.

~ ~ ~

Both paths end in the same place: you have a paper trading account, a watchlist, a live trade with a stop-loss, and a record of what you did and why. The journal is fast and personal. The dashboard is structured, tracks your XP, and builds the trade log you'll analyze in later chapters. Either way, you just went from spectator to player.

Coming Up Next: Scouting the Map

You're in the game. You have a platform, a watchlist, and your first trade live. That's more than most adults can say.

But right now, you probably picked your stocks based on gut feeling - brands you like, names you recognize. That's a fine way to start, but it's not a strategy. In chess, you don't just move pieces randomly. Every move has a reason.

In Chapter 4, we're going to learn how to actually scout and pick stocks like a strategist. You'll learn what makes a good "starter stock," how to read a stock's profile page like a character stats screen, and how different sectors of the market work like different biomes in a game. By the end, you'll build a proper watchlist based on research, not just recognition.

Time to scout the map.

Chapter 4

Scouting the Map - How to Pick Your First Stocks

In chess, you don't just move pieces randomly. Every move has a reason:

A beginner shoves pawns forward and hopes for the best. A smart player studies the board, thinks two or three moves ahead, and chooses each move with intention. The pieces look the same in both games, but the thinking behind them is completely different.

Picking stocks works the same way. In Chapter 3, you placed your first paper trade - and you probably picked a company you already knew and liked. That's perfectly fine for a first move. But from now on, we're going to pick stocks the way a smart chess player picks moves: with a reason, a plan, and a method.

In this chapter, you're going to learn about becoming a smart trader, just like the smart gamer you are. Learn what makes a good starter stock, how to read a stock's profile like a character stats page, how different market sectors work like different biomes in a game, and the most powerful beginner principle in all of investing. By the end, you'll build your first research-backed watchlist of five U.S. stocks.

Time to scout the map. Lets head out!

Choosing Your Starter Characters - What Makes a Good Beginner Stock

Every game gives you starter characters. In Fortnite, you land with a basic loadout. In Pokémon, you pick your first companion from a small, trusted group. These starters aren't the flashiest options, but they're reliable, well-rounded, and designed to help you learn the basics without getting destroyed.

The stock market has starter characters too. They're called **large-cap, blue-chip stocks** - big, well-known American companies that have been around for years, make steady profits, and are traded by millions of people every day.

Here's why they're perfect for beginners:

They're stable. Large-cap companies like Apple, Microsoft, and Johnson & Johnson don't usually swing 20% in a single day. They move in steadier, more predictable ways. That's exactly what you want while you're learning. You don't learn to drive in a Formula 1 car.

They're well-covered. Thousands of analysts, journalists, and investors follow these companies every day. That means there's tons of information available - news articles, earnings reports, YouTube breakdowns. You'll never be short on research material.

They're liquid. "Liquidity" simply means that there's always someone willing to buy and someone willing to sell the company shares. With millions of shares traded daily, you can buy or sell anytime without trouble. Smaller, less popular stocks sometimes don't have enough buyers, which can trap you in a position you can't exit.

You already know them. You use their products every single day. That familiarity is a real advantage, and we'll talk about why in a moment.

Here are some classic beginner-friendly starter stocks on the U.S. market:

Apple (AAPL) - iPhones, MacBooks, AirPods. The most valuable company in the world.

Coca-Cola (KO) - One of the most famous brands in history. Warren Buffett's favorite stock.

Johnson & Johnson (JNJ) - Band-Aids, Tylenol, medical devices. A healthcare giant that's paid dividends for over 60 years.

Microsoft (MSFT) - Windows, Xbox, Teams, Azure cloud. A titan of both software and gaming.

Walmart (WMT) - The largest retailer on Earth. Nearly every American has shopped there.

Walt Disney (DIS) - Theme parks, Marvel, Star Wars, Disney+. Entertainment royalty.

Gamer Tip: You wouldn't start a new game by fighting the final boss. Starter stocks are your training partners. They help you learn without punishing you for small mistakes. Save the risky, volatile picks for later when your skills are sharper.

Reading the Stats Page - How to Check Out a Stock's Profile

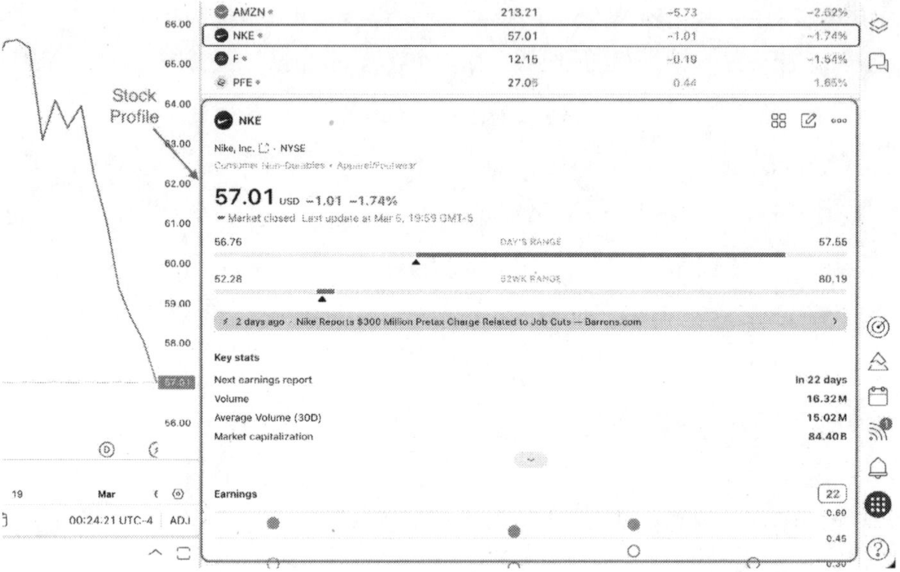

Stock Profile

In any RPG, before you choose a character, you check their stats. Attack power, defense, speed, special abilities - you want to know what you're working with before you commit.

Stocks have a stats page too. Every stock on the market has a profile that shows you its key numbers. You can find it by searching any company on Google, Yahoo Finance, or TradingView. Let's decode the most important stats.

Stock Price

This is the most visible number - what one share costs right now. Apple might show $257. Nike might show $57. But here's something that trips up a lot of beginners: **a higher stock price doesn't mean a better company.**

Amazon's stock price might be $213, while Berkshire Hathaway's Class A shares trade at over $720,000. Does that mean Berkshire Hathaway is thousands of times better? Not necessarily. The price per share depends on how many total shares exist. A company can have a low stock price but a massive total value, or a high stock price and a relatively small total value. The stock price alone doesn't tell you how good a company is. It's just one stat on the page. Lets learn about the other stats to understand a company better.

52-Week High and Low

This shows the highest and lowest prices the stock has reached over the past year. Think of it as the character's peak performance and worst slump over the last season.

If Apple's 52-week high is $288 and its 52-week low is $169, and it's currently trading at $257, you can see it's closer to its highs than its lows. That tells you the stock has been generally strong this past year.

If a stock is sitting right at its 52-week low, it might be a bargain - or it might be in serious trouble. Context matters, and you'll learn to read that context as your skills grow.

P/E Ratio: The Price Tag Checker

The **P/E ratio (Price-to-Earnings ratio)** is one of the most useful stats for any investor. It tells you how expensive a stock is relative to how much money the company actually earns.

Here's the simplest way to think about it. Imagine two lemonade stands. Both sell lemonade at the same stand price of $100. But Stand A earns $10 in profit per year, while Stand B earns $20 in profit per year. Stand A has a P/E of 10 (price ÷ earnings = 100 ÷ 10). Stand B has a P/E of 5.

The lower P/E means you're paying less for each dollar of profit the company generates. Stand B is a better deal - you get more earning power for your money.

In the real market, a P/E of 15–20 is considered average for a large U.S. company. Tech companies like NVIDIA or Amazon often have P/E ratios of 30, 50, or even higher because investors believe their earnings will grow fast in the future. Stable companies like Coca-Cola or Johnson & Johnson tend to have lower P/E ratios because their growth is steadier.

A sky-high P/E isn't automatically bad, and a low P/E isn't automatically good. It's just one stat that tells you how much you're paying for what you're getting. Like checking the price-to-power ratio on a gaming headset before you buy it.

Gamer Translation: Stock price = how much a single copy costs. 52-week high/low = best and worst performance this season. P/E ratio = the value-for-money score. Always check the stats page before you pick your character.

Sectors as Biomes - The Different Worlds of the Stock Market

In Minecraft, you don't find diamonds in the ocean and you don't fish in the desert. Each biome has its own resources, its own dangers, and its own survival strategies. The U.S. stock market works the same way. Companies are grouped into **sectors** - categories based on what kind of business they run. Each sector behaves differently and responds to the world in its own way.

The S&P 500 contains 11 official sectors. You don't need to memorize all of them right now, but knowing the main ones gives you a massive strategic advantage. Here are the ones that matter most for beginners:

Technology - The High-Speed Biome

This is the flashiest, fastest-moving sector. Companies like Apple, Microsoft, NVIDIA, Google (Alphabet), and Meta live here. Tech stocks tend to grow fast but can also drop sharply when the market gets nervous. High reward, higher risk.

If you love innovation and don't mind some turbulence, the tech biome is exciting. Just know that it's the sector most likely to give you a wild ride.

Healthcare - The Defensive Healer Biome

Companies like Johnson & Johnson, UnitedHealth, and Pfizer operate here. People need medicine and healthcare no matter what the economy is doing, which makes this sector more stable than most. Healthcare stocks are the "healer class" of your portfolio - they keep things steady when everything else is taking damage.

Consumer Staples - The Survival Essentials Biome

Coca-Cola, Procter & Gamble, Walmart, Costco - these companies sell things people buy no matter what: food, drinks, toothpaste, household supplies. Even during a recession, people still eat and brush their teeth. Consumer staples stocks are boring but reliable, like carrying a full stack of bread in Minecraft. Not exciting, but it keeps you alive.

Financials - The Banking Empire Biome

JPMorgan Chase, Goldman Sachs, Visa, and Mastercard run the money infrastructure of America. Banks, payment networks, and insurance companies all sit in this sector. Financials tend to do well when the economy is strong and interest rates are rising.

Energy - The Resource Biome

ExxonMobil, Chevron, and ConocoPhillips dominate this sector. They extract, refine, and sell oil, gas, and other energy resources. When oil prices spike, energy stocks soar. When oil crashes, they suffer. This biome is resource-dependent and cyclical - great for experienced traders, trickier for beginners.

Here's the strategic insight: **different sectors perform differently at different times.** When the economy is booming, tech and financials tend to lead. When the economy slows down, healthcare and consumer staples tend to hold up better. This is called **sector rotation**, and we'll explore it deeply in Book 2.

For now, the key takeaway is simple: don't put all your stocks in one biome. Spread your watchlist across at least two or three sectors so you're not overexposed to a single area.

The "Buy What You Know" Principle - Your Secret Advantage

Here's the single most powerful stock-picking idea for beginners, and it comes from one of the greatest investors of all time: Peter Lynch.

Peter Lynch managed the Magellan Fund at Fidelity from 1977 to 1990 and turned it into the best-performing mutual fund in the world. His average annual return was 29%. His secret? He believed ordinary people could find great investments just by paying attention to their everyday lives.

He called it **"Buy what you know."**

The idea is simple. You already interact with dozens of companies every single day. The phone in your pocket (Apple or Samsung). The shoes on your feet (Nike or Adidas). The streaming service you watched last night (Netflix or Disney+). The store where your family buys groceries (Walmart, Costco, or Target). The search engine you use for homework (Google).

You have firsthand experience with these companies. You know if their products are good. You notice when a brand suddenly gets popular at your school. You can tell when a company's app has gotten worse or when a new feature makes everyone excited.

That real-world knowledge is an advantage. Adults sitting in offices reading financial reports don't always know which gaming company is blowing up on Twitch or which sneaker brand just dropped the hottest collab. But you do. You're living in the market every day without even realizing it. So take advantage of it and learn to read the world around you.

How to Put This Into Practice

Grab your journal and try this exercise right now. Think about your typical day and write down every company you interact with:

You wake up and check your phone - **Apple**. You scroll through Instagram - **Meta**. You eat cereal from a brand your parents buy at Walmart - **Walmart** and maybe **General Mills**. You wear Nike sneakers to school - **Nike**. You watch YouTube during lunch - **Google (Alphabet)**. You play

Roblox or games on an NVIDIA-powered PC after school - **Roblox** and **NVIDIA**. Your family orders dinner on DoorDash and pays with a Visa card - **DoorDash** and **Visa**.

In one single day, you've interacted with ten or more publicly traded companies. Each one has a stock you can research, track, and eventually paper trade. You're not picking blind. You're picking from personal experience.

Gamer Tip: "Buy what you know" doesn't mean "buy because you like the brand." It means start your research with companies you understand. Liking a product is step one. Checking the stats page and making sure the numbers look solid is step two. Always do both.

Case Study: Mia Builds Her First Research-Backed Watchlist

Mia is 17 and lives in Seattle. She's already set up TradingView and placed her first paper trade on Apple (from Chapter 3). Now she wants to build a proper watchlist using what she's learned in this chapter.

She starts with the "Buy What You Know" exercise. She grabs her journal and lists the companies she interacts with daily: Apple (phone), Nike (shoes), YouTube/Google (entertainment), Amazon (family orders packages constantly), and Starbucks (her mom's daily habit).

Next, she checks the stats page for each company on Yahoo Finance. She writes down the stock price, 52-week high and low, and P/E ratio for all five.

She notices that Apple's P/E is around 30, which seems fair for a massive tech company. Nike's P/E is around 28. Amazon's P/E is higher at about 60, which tells her investors expect Amazon's earnings to grow a lot in the future. Starbucks has a P/E of about 25, and its stock is near the middle of its 52-week range - not at its peak, not at its bottom.

Finally, she checks which sectors they belong to. Apple and Amazon are in Technology (though Amazon also overlaps with Consumer Discretionary). Nike and Starbucks are in Consumer Discretionary. She realizes four of her five picks are in similar sectors. She's heavy on consumer and tech, with nothing in healthcare, financials, or energy.

To diversify, she swaps one pick. She drops her second Starbucks idea and adds Johnson & Johnson (healthcare) to her watchlist. Now she has three sectors covered instead of two.

Her final watchlist: Apple (Tech), Nike (Consumer), Amazon (Tech/Consumer), Google (Tech), and Johnson & Johnson (Healthcare). Five companies she understands, with stats she's checked, spread across multiple biomes.

Mia didn't just pick names she liked. She scouted the map.

Level 4 Complete - Your Map Is Scouted

You now know how to pick stocks with a purpose instead of guessing. Let's lock in the key lessons:

Start with large-cap, blue-chip stocks. Companies like Apple, Microsoft, Walmart, and Coca-Cola are your starter characters. They're stable, well-covered, and forgiving of beginner mistakes.

Always check the stats page. Stock price tells you the cost, the 52-week range shows recent performance, and the P/E ratio reveals whether you're paying a fair price for the company's earnings.

Think in sectors. Technology, healthcare, consumer staples, financials, and energy are the main biomes. Spread your picks across at least two or three sectors to avoid being wiped out by trouble in one area.

"Buy what you know" is your starting point. Use your daily life to find companies worth researching. Your personal experience is a real advantage - but always back it up by checking the numbers.

Chapter 4 Mission

This is the mission where your watchlist gets serious Pick your path:

Path A: The Journal

Step 1: In your Paper Trading Journal, write down every company you interacted with today. Aim for at least eight. Include the product you used and the company name.

Step 2: From that list, pick five stocks you want to research. Search each one on Yahoo Finance or TradingView. Write down the stock symbol, current price, 52-week high and low, and P/E ratio.

Step 3: Check your sector balance. Write down which sector each stock belongs to. If more than three are in the same sector, swap one out for a company in a different biome.

Step 4: Add all five stocks to your watchlist on TradingView (or your chosen platform). These are the stocks you'll track, study, and eventually paper trade over the coming chapters.

Step 5: Title this page in your journal: "My Starting Five - Version 1.0." Your watchlist will evolve as you learn, and that's a good thing. Version 1.0 is just the beginning.

Mission time: 25 minutes. Difficulty: Medium. XP earned: You now pick stocks like a scout, not a guesser.

Path B: The Mission Log Dashboard

If you want a structured scouting system with XP tracking, open the Paper Trading Boss Battles Mission Log Dashboard. Navigate to Chapter 5: Skill Tree and launch Company Scorecards. Here's what's waiting:

Company Scorecards (+250 XP)-Eight pre-loaded companies span multiple sectors: Apple and Microsoft in Technology, Amazon in Consumer Discretionary, JPMorgan in Financials, Johnson & Johnson in Healthcare, Exxon Mobil in Energy, Procter & Gamble in Staples, and NVIDIA in Technology. Each scorecard has eleven fields: stock price, market cap, P/E ratio, revenue, net income, dividend yield, sector, competitors, strength, risk, and your verdict of Buy, Hold, or Avoid. Fill out three or more scorecards to complete the mission.

Sector Analysis (+250 XP)-Three exercises teach you to think in sectors, not just stocks. Rank eight sector ETFs from strongest to weakest. Compare what was leading thirty days ago to what's leading now. Then pit one of your stocks against its sector ETF to see if it's outperforming or underperforming the group. Complete two of three to earn the XP.

The scorecards give you the same data the journal asks for-price, P/E, sector-plus deeper fields like revenue, competitors, and a final verdict. The sector exercises make sure your roster isn't stacked in one biome. Together, they're the dashboard's version of building your Starting Five.

~ ~ ~

Both paths end with the same result: a researched, sector-balanced watchlist built on real data instead of guesses. The journal is fast and freeform. The dashboard gives you structured scorecards and sector exercises that you'll build on in later books. Whichever you choose, add your picks to TradingView. These are the stocks you'll study and trade from here on out.

Coming Up Next: Understanding the Game Engine

You've got a watchlist of five solid stocks spread across multiple sectors. You know their stats. You know their stories. You picked them with intention.

But here's the next question: why do stock prices actually go up and down? What makes Apple jump 3% on a Tuesday? What causes Nike to drop 5% after a news report? What invisible forces push the market around every single day?

In Chapter 5, we're going to crack open the game engine - the mechanics behind stock price movement. You'll learn about company earnings, news events, Federal Reserve decisions, and the big institutional players (the "whales") who move markets. Once you understand *why* prices move, you'll start seeing the market like a whole new game.

The game engine is waiting. Let's crack it open.

Chapter 5

Understanding the Game Engine - Why Stock Prices Go Up and Down

In Roblox, when a game gets millions of visits, its creator earns more Robux. Stocks work on the same principle.

Popularity, performance, and perception drive everything. A game that delivers great updates attracts more players. A game that breaks and never gets fixed loses them. The creator's income rises or falls based on what people think about the experience.

Stock prices move the same way. When a company performs well, delivers strong results, or excites investors about the future, more people want to buy the stock and the price goes up. When a company disappoints, makes mistakes, or scares people with bad news, investors sell and the price drops.

But it goes deeper than that. Stock prices don't just react to one company's news. They react to the entire world - the economy, government decisions, global events, and even the mood of millions of people making buy-and-sell decisions at the same time.

In this chapter, we're going to crack open the game engine. You'll learn the four main forces that push stock prices up and down every single day. Once you understand these mechanics, you'll stop seeing price movements as random and start seeing them as cause and effect.

Let's look under the hood.

Supply and Demand in Action - The FOMO Rally and the Panic Dump

In Chapter 2, we learned the basic rule: when more people want to buy a stock than sell it, the price goes up. When more people want to sell than buy, the price goes down. That's supply and demand in a sentence.

Now let's see what that looks like in the real world, because supply and demand doesn't always move in calm, gentle waves. Sometimes it explodes.

The FOMO Rally

FOMO stands for **Fear Of Missing Out**, and you've definitely felt it before. Your friends are all playing a new game you haven't tried. Everyone's talking about it. You see clips everywhere. Even though you're not sure you'll like it, you download it anyway because you don't want to be left out.

FOMO rallies work the same way in the stock market. A stock starts going up. People notice. More people buy. The price climbs higher. Even more people see the price climbing and think, "I need to get in before it's too late!" They pile in. The price spikes up even faster.

The problem? FOMO buyers often arrive at the very top. They buy because the price is going up, not because the company is actually worth that much. When the excitement fades, the price crashes back down and the late arrivals are stuck holding an overpriced stock.

GameStop in January 2021 was the most famous FOMO rally in recent history. A group of retail traders on Reddit's WallStreetBets forum began buying GameStop shares and call options, which put pressure on hedge funds that had bet against the stock. GameStop's price rocketed from around $20 to nearly $500 in less than a month. People who had never traded before were opening brokerage accounts just to jump in. But when the frenzy cooled, the stock crashed back to earth. Many latecomers lost huge amounts of money.

The Panic Dump

The opposite of FOMO is panic selling. Bad news hits, fear spreads, and everyone rushes for the exit at the same time - like a server crashing and every player trying to log out simultaneously.

When COVID-19 shut down the global economy in March 2020, the S&P 500 dropped over 30% in about five weeks. Investors were terrified. Businesses closed. Nobody knew how bad things would get. People sold stocks as fast as they could, which pushed prices lower, which scared even more people into selling.

But here's the twist that catches most people off guard: the market bottomed out in late March 2020, and by August it had already recovered to new all-time highs. People who panic-sold at the bottom locked in their losses forever. People who stayed calm - or even bought more during the dip - made some of the best trades of their lives.

Gamer Tip: FOMO and panic are the two emotions that destroy the most money in the stock market. Recognizing them is like learning to spot a trap in a game. Once you see the pattern, you stop falling for it.

The same goes to life. FOMO and panic are the two most influential modes in one's life decision. Be aware of it!

Company Earnings - The Seasonal Updates That Move Stocks

Four times a year, every publicly traded company in America releases its **earnings report**. Think of it as a quarterly report card - or better yet, a seasonal update for a game. The company tells the world: here's how much money we made, here's how much we spent, and here's how we're doing compared to what everyone expected.

Earnings season is one of the most exciting and volatile times in the market. Stock prices can jump 5%, 10%, or even 20% in a single day based on what the report says.

Beating Expectations vs. Missing Them

Before a company reports earnings, Wall Street analysts make predictions about how much money the company will earn. These predictions are called **estimates** or **expectations**. The stock's reaction depends less on the raw numbers and more on whether the company **beat or missed** those expectations.

If Apple is expected to earn $1.50 per share and it reports $1.65, that's a beat. Investors get excited, more buyers flood in, and the stock price jumps. But if Apple reports $1.40 - still profitable, but below what Wall Street predicted - the stock can drop sharply even though the company made money.

This trips up beginners all the time. They see a company report billions in profit and can't understand why the stock went down. The reason is almost always the same: the company made money, but not as much as people expected. In the stock market, **expectations are everything**.

A Real Example: Netflix's Subscriber Surprise

In early 2022, Netflix reported its quarterly earnings and revealed that it had lost subscribers for the first time in over a decade. The actual number wasn't catastrophic - they lost about 200,000 subscribers. But Wall Street had expected Netflix to gain 2.5 million new subscribers. The gap between expectation and reality was massive.

The stock dropped over 35% in a single day. Billions of dollars in market value vanished overnight. Not because Netflix suddenly became a bad company, but because reality didn't match the story investors had been telling themselves.

Earnings season is when the market separates facts from hype. As a paper trader, you'll want to know when your watchlist stocks are reporting earnings so you're not blindsided by a massive move.

Gamer Translation: Earnings reports are like seasonal game updates. A great update (beat expectations) brings players flooding back and the stock price climbs. A disappointing update (missed expectations) causes players to leave and the stock drops. Always check the update schedule.

News and Events - The Game Patches That Change Everything

Beyond earnings, the world itself constantly throws curveballs at the stock market. Government decisions, global events, and big policy changes act like game patches - they can buff certain stocks, nerf others, and completely change the meta overnight.

The Federal Reserve: The Game Developers

The **Federal Reserve (the Fed)** is the central bank of the United States, and it's arguably the single most powerful force in the stock market. If companies are the characters and the stock market is the arena, the Fed is the development team that controls the rules of the game.

The Fed's main tool is **interest rates**. Here's the simplified version: when the Fed lowers interest rates, borrowing money from banks becomes cheaper. Companies can expand more easily, people buy more stuff, and the economy heats up. That's usually great for stocks. When the Fed raises interest rates, borrowing becomes more expensive. Companies slow down, spending cools off, and stock prices often dip.

In 2022 and 2023, the Fed raised interest rates aggressively to fight inflation (rising prices of everyday goods). Tech stocks got hit especially hard because many tech companies depend on cheap borrowing to fund their growth. The NASDAQ, packed with tech names, dropped over 30% from its peak.

Every six weeks or so, the Fed meets to decide whether to raise, lower, or hold interest rates steady. These meetings are called **FOMC meetings** (Federal Open Market Committee), and on those days, the entire stock market holds its breath.

Government Spending and Policy Changes

When the U.S. government passes major spending bills or changes policy, entire sectors can shift. In 2022, the Inflation Reduction Act directed billions of dollars toward clean energy, electric vehicles, and semiconductor manufacturing. Stocks of solar companies, EV makers, and chip producers jumped because investors knew government money was flowing their way.

The opposite happens too. When the government talks about tighter regulations on Big Tech, stocks like Google, Meta, and Amazon can dip on fears that new rules will cut into their profits.

Global Events: The Unexpected Boss Fights

Sometimes events happen that nobody predicted, and the market reacts instantly. Wars, pandemics, natural disasters, and geopolitical crises can send shockwaves through every stock on the board.

When Russia invaded Ukraine in February 2022, energy prices spiked overnight because Russia is a major oil and gas exporter. ExxonMobil and Chevron surged. Meanwhile, European stocks and companies with operations in Russia cratered. One event - one patch to the game world - reshuffled the entire leaderboard.

You can't predict these events. But you can learn to react to them calmly and understand their impact. A disciplined trader doesn't panic when the map changes. They adapt.

The Whales - Big Players Who Move Markets

In every online game, there are whales - players who spend so much money or have so much power that their actions affect everyone else on the server. The stock market has whales too, and they're called **institutional investors**.

These are not individual people buying a few shares of Apple on their phone. These are massive organizations managing billions, sometimes trillions, of dollars:

Hedge funds are private investment firms that use aggressive strategies to beat the market. Names like Bridgewater Associates, Citadel, and Renaissance Technologies manage tens of billions of dollars. When a hedge fund decides to buy or sell a stock, they're moving so much money that their trades alone can push the price.

Mutual funds and index funds are pools of money from millions of everyday investors managed by companies like Vanguard, BlackRock, and Fidelity. Vanguard's S&P 500 index fund alone holds over $800 billion. When these funds rebalance their portfolios, they buy and sell enormous quantities of stock.

Investment banks like Goldman Sachs, JPMorgan, and Morgan Stanley trade stocks on behalf of wealthy clients and corporations. They also publish research reports that thousands of traders follow, which can move markets just by changing a recommendation.

Here's the part that matters for you: institutional investors account for roughly 70–80% of all trading volume on the U.S. stock market. That means the majority of buying and selling isn't being done by regular people - it's being done by these whales.

You can't fight whales head-on. That would be like a level-5 character trying to solo a raid boss. But you can learn to swim in the same direction. When big institutions are buying a stock (you'll learn to spot this through volume, which we cover in Chapter 8), the price tends to go up. When they're selling, it tends to go down. Smart retail traders - that's you - watch the whales and move with them, not against them.

Gamer Tip: You don't need to beat the whales. You just need to notice which direction they're swimming. Tools like trading volume help you see their footprints. We'll cover this in Chapter 8.

Case Study: How One Event Moved Three Stocks in Different Directions

Let's put all four forces together with a real-world example.

In September 2023, the Federal Reserve announced it would hold interest rates steady after months of aggressive hikes. Here's what happened to three stocks on the same day:

Apple (AAPL): Rose about 1.5%. Tech stocks had been beaten down by rising rates, so when the Fed paused, investors saw it as a green light to buy tech again. Demand surged for Apple shares. FOMO kicked in - people didn't want to miss the tech rebound.

Bank of America (BAC): Dropped about 1%. Banks actually benefit from higher interest rates because they can charge more on loans. A pause in rate hikes meant potentially less profit for banks going forward. Institutional investors trimmed their bank holdings.

ExxonMobil (XOM): Barely moved. Energy stocks were more focused on oil prices that day than on the Fed's decision. Different sectors respond to different forces. Not every stock dances to the same tune.

One event. Three stocks. Three completely different reactions. That's the game engine in action. Supply and demand, earnings expectations, news events, and institutional behavior all collide at once, and the result is the price movement you see on your screen.

The more you watch the market, the more these patterns start to click. That's why paper trading is so powerful - you get to watch the engine run without any financial risk.

Level 5 Complete - You See the Engine Now

You've cracked open the game engine and seen how it works. Price movements aren't random - they're driven by real forces that you can learn to read.

Here's what to carry forward:

Supply and demand creates the moves. FOMO rallies happen when everyone piles in at once. Panic dumps happen when fear takes over. Both are emotional extremes, and recognizing them early is a superpower.

Earnings reports are the quarterly report cards. Stocks react to whether a company beat or missed expectations, not just whether it made money. Always know when your watchlist stocks are reporting.

News and the Fed are the game patches. Interest rate decisions, government spending bills, and global events can reshuffle the entire market overnight. You can't predict them, but you can learn to adapt.

Institutional investors are the whales. Hedge funds, mutual funds, and investment banks control roughly 70–80% of trading volume. Swim with the whales, not against them.

Chapter 5 Mission

Path A: The Journal

Step 1: Open your Paper Trading Journal. Pick one stock from your watchlist that had a noticeable price move this past week (up or down). Search for news about that company and write down what caused the move. Was it earnings? A news event? A broader market shift?

Step 2: Search "next FOMC meeting date" on Google. Write the date in your journal and mark it on your calendar. On that day, check what the Fed decides and see how the market reacts. Watch the S&P 500, a tech stock, and a bank stock. Do they all move the same way?

Step 3: Find your watchlist stocks' next earnings dates. Search each company name followed by "earnings date" on Google. Write the dates in your journal so you're never surprised by a sudden big move.

Step 4: In your journal, write one sentence answering this question: "If the Fed raises interest rates next month, which stock on my watchlist would probably benefit, and which one would probably get hurt?" This is your first attempt at thinking like a strategist, not just a spectator.

Mission time: 20 minutes. Difficulty: Medium. XP earned: You can now form a basic hypothesis about why a stock moved.

Path B: The Mission Log Dashboard

If you want guided research with built-in structure, open the Paper Trading Boss Battles Mission Log Dashboard. Navigate to Chapter 5: Skill Tree and complete these two missions:

Macro Economics (+200 XP)-Four forces that move the entire stock market, each with four research questions. The Fed·Rate Decision panel asks for the current rate, direction, stock impact, and which sectors feel it most. Inflation covers the current CPI, its trend, the Fed's likely response, and consumer impact. Earnings Season asks when the next one starts, what happens on beats and misses, and how to adjust your trading. The Jobs Report covers the latest numbers, market reaction, and how employment connects to Fed policy. Analyse three of the four events to complete the mission.

Sector Analysis (+250 XP)-Eight sector ETFs are displayed as a reference panel: XLK for Technology, XLF for Financials, XLV for Healthcare, and five more. Three exercises follow. Rank all eight from strongest to weakest. Compare the top three now versus thirty days ago to spot rotation. Then compare one stock against its sector ETF to see if it's leading or lagging. Complete two of three to earn the XP.

~ ~ ~

Both paths train the same skill: reading what's under the price. The journal has you research one move, track the Fed, and log earnings dates. The dashboard walks you through all four macro forces with structured prompts and adds sector-level analysis on top. Either way, you stop guessing and start understanding the engine.

Coming Up Next: Your First Weapon

You now understand the engine that moves stock prices. You know about supply and demand, earnings, the Fed, global events, and the whales. You can look at a price move and start forming a theory about why it happened.

But so far, you've been looking at the market through words and headlines. In Chapter 6, we're going to give you your first real weapon: the ability to read stock charts.

Charts are the visual history of everything we've discussed - every earnings reaction, every FOMO rally, every panic dump, every Fed decision - all captured in lines and candles on a screen. A chess grandmaster doesn't just look at the current position - they see patterns. Stock charts let you see patterns too.

Your first weapon is waiting. Let's pick it up.

Chapter 6

Your First Weapon - Reading Basic Stock Charts

A CHESS GRANDMASTER DOESN'T JUST LOOK AT THE CURRENT POSITION - THEY SEE PATTERNS.

They look at the board and see the last twenty moves reflected in where every piece sits right now. They spot formations. They recognize setups they've studied a thousand times before. The position tells a story, and the grandmaster can read it.

A stock chart does the same thing. Every green candle, every red candle, every spike and dip on that chart is a record of real human decisions - thousands of people buying and selling, reacting to earnings reports, Fed announcements, and breaking news. The chart captures the entire story of a stock's price history in one visual.

Up until now, you've been learning the market through words: vocabulary, headlines, company profiles. That's important. But starting today, you're picking up your first real weapon. You're going to learn to read stock charts - the visual language of the market. And once you can read a chart, you see the game completely differently.

Let's arm up.

What Is a Stock Chart and Why It Matters

A stock chart is a visual map of a stock's price over time. The horizontal axis (the bottom) shows time - days, weeks, months, or years. The vertical axis (the right side) shows price. Together, they create a picture of where the stock has been.

Think of it as **replay mode**. After a competitive match in Fortnite or Valorant, you can watch the replay to see exactly what happened and when. A stock chart is the replay of every trading session. It shows you when buyers were winning, when sellers took over, when a big piece of news hit, and how the crowd reacted.

Why does this matter? Because price patterns repeat. Not perfectly, not every time, but often enough that traders have been using charts to make decisions for over a hundred years. When you learn to read a chart, you're not predicting the future - you're recognizing familiar patterns and using them to make smarter, better-informed trades.

Open TradingView right now and search for "AAPL" (Apple). Look at the chart on your screen. That squiggly, colorful display is about to become your best friend.

Two Ways to See the Battle - Line Charts vs. Candlestick Charts

There are two main types of stock charts you'll encounter. One is simple. The other gives you much more information. Both are useful, and TradingView lets you switch between them with one click.

The Line Chart: The Simple View

Line Chart

A **line chart** is the most basic chart type. It draws a single line connecting the closing price of the stock each day (or each hour, or each minute, depending on your timeframe). It looks clean, smooth, and easy to read.

Imagine tracking your score in a video game over time. Every day, you write down your rank at the end of the session and connect the dots. You'd end up with a line that shows your overall trajectory - climbing, falling, or staying flat. That's exactly what a line chart does for a stock's price.

Line charts are great for seeing the big picture at a glance. Is the stock trending up over the past six months? Trending down? Moving sideways? The line makes that obvious.

The limitation? A line chart only shows you one number per time period - the closing price. It hides what happened during the day. A stock might have swung wildly between $180 and $200 before closing at $190, and the line chart would just show you $190. It misses the drama.

The Candlestick Chart: The Detailed Battle Map

Candlestick Chart

This is where things get powerful. A **candlestick chart** shows you four pieces of information for each time period: the opening price, the closing price, the highest price reached, and the lowest price reached. All four data points packed into one small shape called a "candle."

Each candle has two parts. The **body** is the thick middle section. It shows the range between the opening price and the closing price. The **wicks** (also called shadows) are the thin lines above and below the body. They show the highest and lowest prices the stock reached during that period.

Here's the color code that makes candlesticks instantly readable:

Green candle: The stock closed higher than it opened. Buyers won that round. The bottom of the body is the opening price and the top is the closing price. Green = the bulls were in charge.

Red candle: The stock closed lower than it opened. Sellers won that round. The top of the body is the opening price and the bottom is the closing price. Red = the bears took control.

Look at any candlestick chart and you'll see a sequence of green and red candles telling you the day-by-day battle between buyers and sellers. A run of green candles means buyers have been winning consistently - bullish momentum. A streak of red candles means sellers have been dominating - bearish pressure.

Gamer Translation: Line chart = the match summary showing your final score. Candlestick chart = the full replay with every round, every skirmish, every momentum swing. Both are useful, but the candlestick chart gives you the real story.

Try It Right Now

On TradingView, pull up Apple's chart. At the top of the chart, you'll see a small icon next to indicators that lets you change the chart type. Switch between "Line" and "Candles." Notice how the candle view gives you so much more detail? You can see the tug-of-war between buyers and sellers on each individual day.

From this point forward, we'll use candlestick charts as our default. They're the standard tool for traders worldwide, and every concept we cover in the rest of this book builds on them.

Choosing Your Zoom Level - Timeframes Explained

Every chart lets you choose a **timeframe** - how much time each candle represents. This is like choosing how far to zoom in or out on a map.

Different zoom levels show you completely different views of the same stock.

The 1-Day Chart: A Single Match

When you set your timeframe to "1 Day," each candle on the chart represents one full trading day. A one-day chart showing the past month will have roughly 20–22 candles (one for each trading day, since markets are closed on weekends).

This is your bread-and-butter view. It's detailed enough to spot short-term patterns but zoomed out enough to see the bigger trend. Think of it as watching one match - you see every round, every play, every shift in momentum.

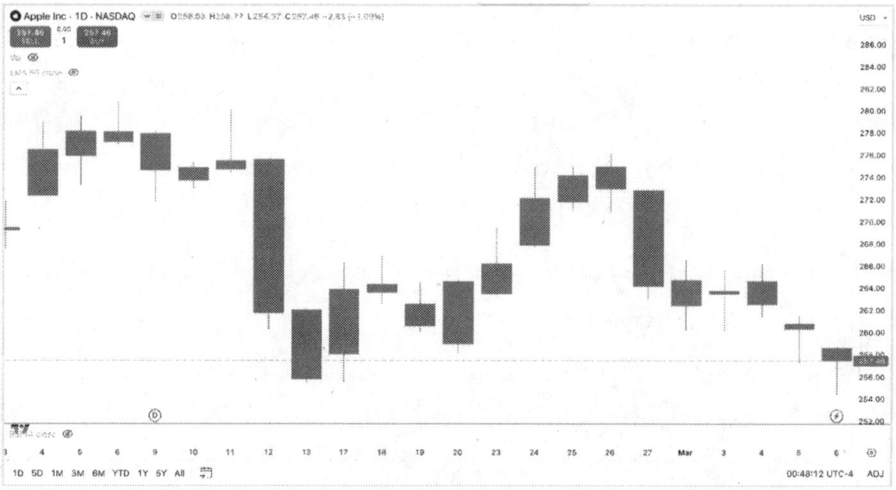

1-Day Chart

The 1-Week Chart: A Tournament

When you switch to a "1 Week" timeframe, each candle now represents one full week of trading compressed into a single shape. A weekly chart showing the past year will have about 52 candles.

The weekly chart smooths out the day-to-day noise and shows you the bigger trends. Small daily drops that seemed scary on the 1-day chart often disappear entirely on the weekly view. It's like watching the highlights of an entire tournament instead of every individual match - you see who's winning overall.

1-Week Chart

The 1-Month Chart: The Full Season

The "1 Month" timeframe compresses each month into one candle. A monthly chart showing five years gives you about 60 candles, and it reveals the longest-term trends. Is the stock in a multi-year uptrend? Has it been flat for three years? Did it crash and recover? The monthly chart answers these big-picture questions.

Think of it as the full season review. You're not looking at individual plays anymore - you're seeing the entire arc of the story.

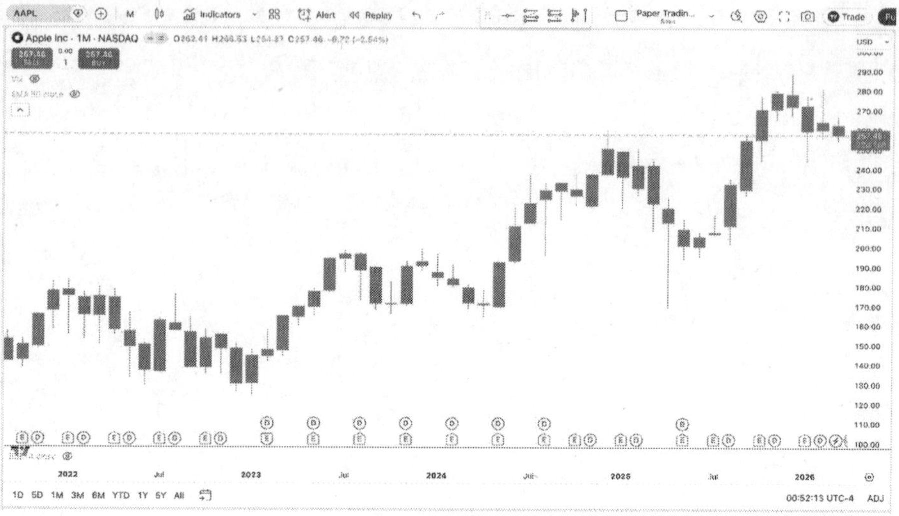

1-Month Chart

Shorter Timeframes: The Minute-by-Minute View

You can also set timeframes to 1 minute, 5 minutes, 15 minutes, or 1 hour. These show you the ultra-zoomed-in action that day traders watch. Each candle represents just a few minutes of trading.

For now, stay away from these. Minute-level charts move fast, create a lot of noise, and can trick beginners into making impulsive decisions. They're useful later when you're more experienced, but at this stage they'll do more harm than good.

Stick with the **daily chart** as your primary view and the **weekly chart** as your backup for big-picture context. That combo gives you everything a beginner needs.

Gamer Tip: Daily chart = watching each match play by play. Weekly chart = tournament highlights. Monthly chart = season recap. Minute charts = watching individual mouse clicks in real time. Not useful until you're way more advanced.

Reading the Battlefield - Uptrends, Downtrends, and Sideways Ranges

Now that you can see candles and choose timeframes, it's time to learn the single most important skill in chart reading: **identifying the trend**.

A trend is simply the general direction a stock's price is moving over time. There are only three possibilities.

Uptrend: The Winning Streak

A stock is in an **uptrend** when its price is making a pattern of **higher highs and higher lows**. That means each peak is higher than the last peak, and each dip is shallower than the last dip. The overall direction is upward, like climbing a staircase.

Think of a team on a winning streak. They might lose a game here and there (the dips), but the overall trajectory is upward - they keep reaching new ranks. Apple from 2019 to 2021 was a textbook uptrend. The stock went from roughly $75 to over $180, making consistent higher highs and higher lows along the way.

What it means for a trader: Uptrends are your best friend. When a stock is in an uptrend, buying on dips (the temporary pullbacks) tends to work well because the overall direction favors the bulls.

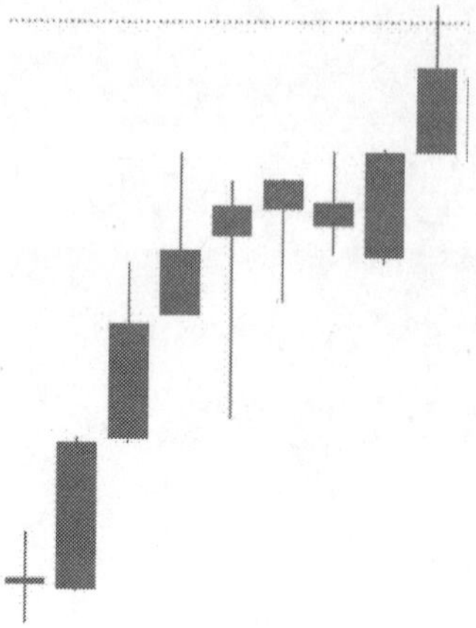

Uptrend

Downtrend: The Losing Streak

A **downtrend** is the opposite. The price makes **lower highs and lower lows**. Each bounce is weaker than the last, and each drop goes deeper. The staircase goes downward.

Netflix in early 2022 was a painful downtrend. After peaking near $700 in late 2021, it started making lower highs and lower lows, eventually falling below $180. Every time it bounced, sellers pushed it back down to an even lower level.

What it means for a trader: Downtrends are dangerous territory for beginners. Trying to buy a stock in a clear downtrend is called "catching a falling knife," and it's exactly as painful as it sounds. Until you're more advanced, avoid trading stocks in strong downtrends.

Downtrend

Sideways Range: The Stalemate

Sometimes a stock isn't going up or down - it's bouncing between the same high point and low point over and over. This is called a **sideways range** or **consolidation**.

Picture a chess game where both players are equally matched. The pieces shuffle back and forth, but neither side gains real ground. That's a sideways range. The stock might bounce between $95 and $105 for weeks, unable to break higher or fall lower.

What it means for a trader: Sideways ranges are waiting zones. The stock is building energy for its next big move. When it finally breaks out of the range (up or down), that breakout can be powerful. We'll cover breakout trading in detail in Book 3.

Sideways

Gamer Translation: Uptrend = winning streak. Downtrend = losing streak. Sideways range = stalemate. Always know which one your stock is in before you trade it. Trading with the trend is like swimming with the current - fighting it is exhausting and usually doesn't end well.

Case Study: Jaylen Reads His First Five Charts

Jaylen is 17 and lives in Atlanta. He set up his TradingView account in Chapter 3 and built his watchlist in Chapter 4: Apple, Nike, Microsoft, Coca-Cola, and Amazon. Now he pulls up each chart on the daily timeframe and reads the trend.

Apple (AAPL): He sees a pattern of higher highs and higher lows over the past three months. Green candles outnumber red ones. The stock is in a clear uptrend. He writes in his journal: "Apple - Uptrend. Bullish."

Nike (NKE): The chart shows a series of lower highs over the past two months. Each bounce gets weaker. Jaylen labels it: "Nike - Downtrend. Stay away for now."

Microsoft (MSFT): Similar to Apple. Steady march upward with occasional small dips. He writes: "Microsoft - Uptrend. Strong."

Coca-Cola (KO): The price has been bouncing between $58 and $62 for about six weeks. No clear direction. He writes: "Coca-Cola - Sideways range. Waiting."

Amazon (AMZN): Uptrend on the weekly chart, but looking at the daily chart, he notices it's pulled back a little in the last few days. He writes: "Amazon - Uptrend overall, short-term pullback." He marks it as a stock to watch for a potential buying opportunity.

In fifteen minutes, Jaylen built a clear picture of all five stocks on his watchlist. He knows which ones are trending up, which one to avoid, which is stuck in a range, and which might offer a buying opportunity soon. He didn't need a finance degree. He just needed candles, a timeframe, and the ability to spot the staircase.

Level 6 Complete - Your First Weapon Is Equipped

You now have a skill that most adults never develop: the ability to look at a stock chart and read what it's telling you. Let's lock in the essentials:

A stock chart is replay mode. It's a visual history of every battle between buyers and sellers. Learning to read it gives you a massive edge over people who just guess.

Candlestick charts are your default weapon. Each candle shows the open, close, high, and low. Green means buyers won. Red means sellers won. The body tells you the story, the wicks show the extremes.

Timeframes control your zoom level. Stick with the daily chart as your main view and the weekly chart for big-picture context. Avoid minute-level charts for now.

Every stock is in one of three modes. Uptrend (higher highs and higher lows), downtrend (lower highs and lower lows), or sideways range. Always identify the trend before making a trade.

Chapter 6 Mission

Path A: The Journal

Step 1: Open TradingView and pull up each of the five stocks on your watchlist. Switch the chart type to "Candles" if it isn't already. Set the timeframe to "1 Day."

Step 2: For each stock, determine whether it's in an uptrend, downtrend, or sideways range. Look for the staircase pattern: higher highs and higher lows (up), lower highs and lower lows (down), or bouncing between the same levels (sideways).

Step 3: In your Paper Trading Journal, create a "Chart Scan" page. For each stock, write the name, the date, the current price, and your trend call (uptrend / downtrend / sideways). This is the beginning of your chart reading practice.

Step 4: Now switch each chart to the "1 Week" timeframe. Does the bigger picture confirm your daily trend call, or does it show something different? Write down any differences. This teaches you to check multiple zoom levels before forming an opinion.

Step 5: Pick the one stock on your watchlist that's in the clearest uptrend. If you haven't already placed a paper trade on it, consider doing so. You're now trading with the trend behind you.

Mission time: 20 minutes. Difficulty: Medium. XP earned: You can now read a stock chart and identify the trend.

Path B: The Mission Log Dashboard

If you want structured chart exercises with guided prompts, open the Paper Trading Boss Battles Mission Log Dashboard. Navigate to Chapter 4: Beginner Missions and launch Chart Reading.

Chart Reading Exercises (+250 XP)-Five exercises, each color-coded and focused on a different skill. Identify Trend asks you to call SPY's three-month direction and provide evidence. Support and Resistance has you find key levels on any stock and record the prices. Read Candlesticks asks you to find one bullish and one bearish candle and explain what the buyers and sellers did. Volume Check has you find a move of two percent or more and determine whether volume confirmed it. The 50-Day Moving

Average exercise asks you to check three stocks and note whether each is trading above or below the line. Complete four of the five to earn the XP.

Each exercise has its own input fields-dropdowns for trend direction, text fields for tickers and price levels, and open text areas for your analysis. The dashboard saves everything so you can review your chart reads later and see how accurate your early calls were.

~ ~ ~

Both paths build the same muscle: reading a chart and making a call. The journal has you scan your full watchlist across two timeframes and pick the best trend trade. The dashboard breaks chart reading into five focused exercises covering trends, support and resistance, candlesticks, volume, and moving averages. One is freeform, one is guided-both turn you into a chart reader.

Coming Up Next: Walls and Floors

You can read candles. You can spot trends. You're already seeing the market differently than you did just a few chapters ago.

But here's the next piece of the puzzle: stock prices don't just trend smoothly in one direction. They bounce. They hit invisible ceilings and floors where the price keeps getting turned around. These levels have names - Support and Resistance - they are key concepts in trading, and understanding them is super important. Knowing where these levels are can help you predict whether a stock will rise or fall once they're broken.

In Minecraft, bedrock is the floor you can't break through. In Fortnite, your builds create walls enemies can't pass. Stocks have invisible walls and floors too, and in Chapter 7, you're going to learn to see them.

The walls and floors are waiting. Let's find them.

Chapter 7

Walls and Floors - Support, Resistance, and Price Levels

In Minecraft, bedrock is the floor you can't break through. In Fortnite, your builds create walls enemies can't pass.

Every game has boundaries - hard surfaces where movement stops, floors that catch you when you fall, and ceilings that block you from climbing higher. You learn to spot them instinctively. You know that bedrock is as deep as you can dig. You know that a reinforced wall will hold for a few more hits before it breaks.

Stocks have invisible walls and floors too. They're not coded into the game by a developer - they're created by the collective behavior of millions of traders. And once you learn to see them, they become one of the most powerful tools in your entire trading arsenal.

These walls and floors have names: **support** and **resistance**. They're the foundation of how traders decide when to buy, when to sell, and when to wait. This chapter is going to teach you to see them on any chart, draw them yourself, and use them to make smarter paper trades.

Let's find the walls and floors.

Support - The Floor That Catches the Fall

Support

Imagine you're bouncing a basketball on a gym floor. Every time the ball drops, it hits the floor and bounces back up. The floor doesn't let it fall any further. If you kept dropping the ball from the same height and force, it would keep bouncing off that same spot, over and over.

That's exactly how **support** works on a stock chart. A support level is a specific **price** where buyers consistently step in and start buying. Every time the stock drops to that price, enough people decide "that's a good deal" and start buying, which pushes the price back up.

Here's a real example. Imagine Apple's stock drops from $195 to $180, and then buyers flood in and push it back up to $192. A few weeks later, Apple dips again - and once again, it stops falling right around $180 and bounces. Then it happens a third time. Each time the price hits $180, it catches like a ball hitting the floor.

That $180 level is now a clear **support level**. Traders around the world can see it on their charts. They know that every time Apple reaches $180, buyers have shown up. That gives them confidence to buy near that price, because history suggests the floor will hold.

Why Does Support Form?

Support levels form because of human psychology - and it's simpler than you'd think.

When a stock drops to a certain price and then bounces, everyone who bought near that low point feels smart. They got a good deal. The next time the stock approaches that same price, those same people - and others who saw what happened - want to buy again at that "proven" level. Meanwhile, people who already own the stock and saw it bounce before feel less panicked about selling, because they trust the floor will hold.

The result is a **wall** of buying demand at that price. More buyers step in, fewer sellers are willing to dump, and the stock bounces. It's a self-reinforcing pattern. The more times a support level holds, the stronger it becomes in traders' minds.

Gamer Translation: Support is like bedrock in Minecraft. No matter how hard the stock falls, it keeps hitting this floor and bouncing back up. The more times it bounces, the more traders trust it.

Resistance - The Ceiling That Blocks the Climb

Resistance

Now flip the picture. If support is the floor, **resistance** is the ceiling.

A resistance level is a specific **price** where sellers consistently step in and start selling. Every time the stock rises to that price, enough people decide "that's high enough, I'm taking my profit" and start selling, which pushes the price back down.

Let's say Microsoft rises from $380 to $410, and then it stalls. Sellers take over, and the price drops back to $395. A few weeks later, Microsoft rallies again - and once more, it stalls right around $410 and falls back. Then it happens a third time. Every time the stock approaches $410, it hits an invisible ceiling and gets turned away.

That $410 level is now a clear **resistance level**. Traders can see it plain as day on their charts. They know that every time Microsoft reaches that zone, sellers show up and push the price down.

Why Does Resistance Form?

The psychology is the mirror image of support.

When a stock rises to a certain price and then falls, people who bought near the top feel trapped. They're holding a stock that dropped right after they bought it. What do they want more than anything? To get back to their buy price so they can sell and escape without a loss. That's called **"breaking even."**

So the next time the stock approaches that same price, all those trapped buyers start selling to break even. At the same time, traders who rode the stock up from lower levels see the previous high on the chart and decide to take profits before the ceiling rejects the price again.

The result is a **wall** of selling pressure at that price. More sellers appear, buyers get cautious, and the stock gets pushed back down. Just like support, the more times a resistance level holds, the stronger it becomes.

Gamer Translation: Resistance is like a build wall in Fortnite. Every time the stock tries to push through, sellers smack it back down. It takes a powerful move to finally break through.

Drawing the Lines - How to Find Support and Resistance on Any Chart

Finding support and resistance isn't some advanced wizard skill. It's pattern recognition, and you're about to learn the exact steps. All you need is a candlestick chart on TradingView and the horizontal line drawing tool.

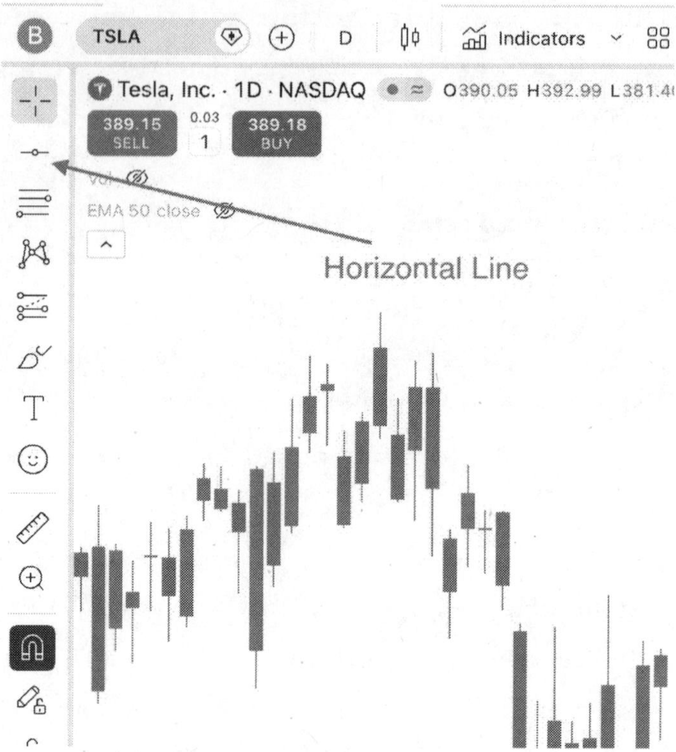

Horizontal Line

Step-by-Step: Finding and Drawing Support

Step 1: Open a daily candlestick chart of any stock on your watchlist in TradingView.

Step 2: Look for areas where the price dropped and then bounced back up. Focus on the low points - the bottoms of the dips.

Step 3: Look for two or more dips that bottomed out at roughly the same price. They don't need to be exactly the same penny - within a dollar or two counts. If you see the stock bouncing off the same general area multiple times, that's your support zone.

Step 4: Select the horizontal line tool on TradingView (it's in the left toolbar under drawing tools). Click on the price level where those bounces occurred. You've just drawn a support line.

Step-by-Step: Finding and Drawing Resistance

Step 1: On the same chart, look for areas where the price rose and then got rejected - pushed back down.

Step 2: Find two or more peaks that topped out at roughly the same price. These are the spots where sellers consistently showed up.

Step 3: Draw a horizontal line at that price level. That's your resistance line.

Now step back and look at your chart. You should see horizontal lines that create a visual channel - a floor below and a ceiling above. The stock is bouncing between these two walls. That visual is incredibly powerful. In seconds, you can see exactly where buyers and sellers are fighting for control.

Support & Resistance

The Golden Rule: Zones, Not Exact Lines

Here's an important nuance that separates smart chart readers from rigid ones: support and resistance are **zones**, not exact lines. The price won't bounce off $491 on the dot every single time. It might bounce at $489 one day, $487 the next, and $490 the time after that.

Think of it as a general area, not a laser-precise boundary. If you expect perfection, you'll get frustrated and think the tool doesn't work. If you think in zones, you'll see it working everywhere.

Gamer Tip: Support and resistance lines are guidelines, not guarantees. They're like the edges of a capture zone in a game - the action clusters around the area, but individual plays happen slightly inside or outside the boundary.

When the Wall Breaks - Understanding Breakouts

Walls and floors hold until they don't. And when they finally break, something exciting happens.

A **breakout** occurs when a stock's price pushes through a support or resistance level with enough force that it doesn't bounce back. The invisible wall shatters, and the stock enters new territory - like breaking through a barrier in a game and reaching a whole new area.

Resistance Breakout: New Highs Ahead

When a stock breaks above resistance, it means the sellers who kept pushing the price down have finally been overwhelmed by buyers. The buying pressure was just too strong. Once the ceiling breaks, there's no more overhead selling pressure, and the stock often surges higher.

Amazon spent much of late 2023 trading below $145 - a resistance level it couldn't crack. Every rally got rejected near that zone. Then in December, fueled by strong holiday sales data and AI optimism, Amazon finally smashed through $145 with heavy volume. Within weeks, it was trading above $155 and kept climbing. The old ceiling was gone, and a new chapter began.

Resistance Breakout

Support Breakdown: Danger Below

The opposite is a **support breakdown**. When a stock falls through a support level, it means the buyers who kept showing up at that price have been overwhelmed by sellers. The floor collapses, and the stock can fall rapidly to the next support level below.

This is why stop-losses matter. If you bought a stock near a support level and that support breaks, your stop-loss automatically gets you out before the drop accelerates. Without a stop-loss, you'd watch helplessly as the floor disappears.

Support Breakdown

The Role Reversal Trick

Here's one of the coolest concepts in chart reading: when a resistance level breaks, it often becomes the new support level. And when a support level breaks, it often becomes the new resistance.

Think about it logically. Microsoft kept getting rejected at $410 (resistance). Then it finally breaks through and trades at $420. If the price pulls back toward $410 again, all the traders who missed the breakout want a second chance to buy. That old resistance level now has a crowd of buyers waiting at it. The ceiling becomes the new floor.

The same works in reverse. If Apple's support at $180 breaks and the stock falls to $170, that old $180 level now becomes resistance. People who bought at $180 and are underwater want to sell if the price ever comes back to their break-even point. The floor becomes the new ceiling.

Gamer Translation: A breakout is like smashing through a wall into a new zone. Once you're through, the broken wall switches sides - what used to block you now protects you. Old resistance becomes new support.

Old support becomes new resistance. It's one of the most reliable tricks in trading.

Case Study: Sofia's First Support Trade

Sofia is 19 and lives in Phoenix. She's been paper trading for two weeks and has five stocks on her watchlist. Today she decides to practice finding support and resistance.

She pulls up Coca-Cola (KO) on TradingView. On the daily chart, she notices something clear: over the past two months, the stock has dropped to around $58 three separate times, and each time it bounced back up toward $62. She draws a horizontal line at $58. That's her support level.

She also sees that $62 has acted as a ceiling. The stock rallied to that area twice and got pushed back down both times. She draws a second horizontal line at $62. That's resistance.

Now Coca-Cola is sitting at $58.50 - right near support. Sofia thinks: "The floor has held three times already. If it holds again, the stock could bounce back toward $62. That's a potential gain of about $3.50 per share."

She places a paper trade: buys 50 shares of Coca-Cola at $58.50. Then she sets a stop-loss at $57 - just below the support zone. If the floor breaks, she's out automatically with a small loss instead of a big one.

Her plan is simple: if Coca-Cola bounces to $62, she'll sell and take profit. If it breaks below $57, her stop-loss protects her. Either way, she has a plan before the trade plays out.

Four days later, Coca-Cola bounces off $58 again and climbs to $61.40. Sofia sells and books a profit of $2.90 per share - $145 on her 50 shares. Not life-changing money (and it's virtual anyway), but the process was perfect. She identified support, bought near the floor, set a stop-loss below it, and took profit near resistance.

That's what trading with structure looks like. She didn't guess. She read the walls and floors.

Level 7 Complete - You Can See the Walls and Floors

You've added a serious upgrade to your toolkit. Let's lock in the key lessons:

Support is the floor. It's the price level where buyers consistently step in and push the price back up. The more times it holds, the stronger the level. Buying near support is one of the most reliable beginner strategies.

Resistance is the ceiling. It's the price level where sellers consistently step in and push the price back down. Knowing where resistance sits helps you set realistic profit targets.

Draw them as zones, not exact lines. Support and resistance are areas, not laser-precise numbers. Look for clusters of bounces, not a single touch.

Breakouts change the game. When a level finally breaks, the stock enters new territory. And broken walls switch roles - old resistance becomes new support, and old support becomes new resistance.

Chapter 7 Mission

Path A: The Journal

Step 1: Open TradingView and pull up each of your five watchlist stocks on the daily timeframe.

Step 2: For each stock, identify at least one support level and one resistance level. Look for prices where the stock bounced at least twice from the bottom (support) or got rejected at least twice from the top (resistance).

Step 3: Use TradingView's horizontal line drawing tool to mark these levels on each chart. Use green for support and red for resistance if your platform allows color choices.

Step 4: In your Paper Trading Journal, create a "Walls and Floors" page. For each stock, write the name, the support level, the resistance level, and where the current price sits relative to both.

Step 5: Pick one stock that's currently near its support level. Place a paper trade at or near support, and set your stop-loss just below the support zone. Write down your plan: where you'll buy, where you'll exit for profit (near resistance), and where your stop-loss sits.

Mission time: 25 minutes. Difficulty: Medium-Hard. XP earned: You can now read price levels and place trades with a structural reason.

Path B: The Mission Log Dashboard

If you want structured exercises and a digital record, open the Paper Trading Boss Battles Mission Log Dashboard. Two missions across two chapters cover exactly what this chapter asks:

Chart Reading - Support & Resistance (+250 XP)-Navigate to Chapter 4: Beginner Missions and open Chart Reading. The second exercise is Support & Resistance. Enter any ticker, then record every level you find with exact prices-where buying has prevented decline and where selling has prevented a rise. This is one of five exercises in the Chart Reading set, and completing four of five earns the full XP.

Log Trades (+250 XP)-Once you've placed your paper trade at support, navigate to Chapter 2: Trade Log and open Log Trades. Record your entry price, stop-loss, and target. The dashboard adds fields for confluence signals, emotional state, and plan compliance that you'll use to review this trade later.

If you completed the Trading Rules mission in Chapter 1, you already set rule number two: "Stop at ___ level." This is where that rule comes alive. Your stop goes just below support-a technical level, not a random number.

~ ~ ~

Both paths build the same skill: identifying where price has bounced or stalled, then using those levels to plan a trade. The journal gives you a freeform Walls and Floors page. The dashboard gives you a structured exercise for levels and a trade log for the trade you place at support. Either way, your trades now have a structural reason.

Coming Up Next: Power-Ups Unlocked

You can read candles. You can spot trends. You can see the invisible walls and floors that most people never notice. Your chart-reading skills are growing fast.

But what if you could add tools to your chart that act like a built-in radar - tools that help you confirm whether a trend is real, whether a stock is exhausted, and whether the crowd is truly behind a move? Those tools exist, and they're called **indicators**.

In Chapter 8, we're unlocking three beginner-friendly power-ups: Moving Averages (your trend compass), Volume (the crowd meter), and RSI (the energy bar). They don't predict the future, but they tilt the odds in your favor. Think of them as the radar, the compass, and the health bar that upgrade your entire HUD.

Your power-ups are waiting. Let's unlock them.

Chapter 8

Power-Ups Unlocked - Simple Indicators That Help You Trade

WHAT IF YOUR GAME HAD A BUILT-IN RADAR THAT SHOWED YOU WHERE ENEMIES ARE LIKELY TO GO NEXT?

Not a crystal ball. Not a cheat. Just a tool that takes all the information already on the screen and highlights the patterns you might miss with your naked eye. A compass that shows the direction of the trend. A crowd meter that tells you whether a move is real or fake. An energy bar that warns you when a stock is running out of steam.

Those tools exist in the stock market, and they're called **indicators**. They're mathematical calculations applied to price and volume data, and they appear as lines, bars, or numbers overlaid directly on your chart. Traders have used them for decades to confirm their ideas, filter out noise, and avoid bad trades.

Here's the critical thing to understand before we go any further: **indicators do not predict the future.** Nobody and nothing can do that. What indicators do is tilt the odds in your favor. They help you make better-informed decisions based on what has already happened and what is most likely - not guaranteed - to happen next.

In this chapter, you're unlocking three beginner-friendly power-ups that you'll use for the rest of your trading journey. Let's add them to your loadout.

Power-Up #1: Moving Averages - Your Trend Compass

Imagine you're hiking through a forest and the trail keeps twisting and turning. You can't tell if you're generally heading north or south because every few steps the direction changes. Now imagine pulling out a compass. It doesn't care about the twists. It shows you the overall direction.

A **Moving Average (MA)** is your trend compass. It takes the stock's closing prices over a set number of days, averages them, and draws a smooth line on the chart. That line cuts through the daily noise and shows you the stock's true direction.

How It Works

A **50-day Moving Average** takes the closing price from each of the last 50 trading days, adds them up, and divides by 50. Each new day, it drops the oldest price and adds the newest one, so the line is always "moving" forward. The result is a smooth, flowing line that follows the stock's price on the chart.

There's also the **200-day Moving Average**, which averages the last 200 days. Because it uses more data, it moves more slowly and shows you the very long-term trend.

Moving Average 50 & 200

How to Read It

The rule is beautifully simple:

If the stock's price is above the 50-day MA, the trend is your ally. The stock is generally heading up. Buyers are in control. This is where you want to look for buying opportunities.

If the stock's price is below the 50-day MA, caution is warranted. The stock is trending down or losing momentum. Sellers are gaining the upper hand. This is a zone where beginners should be careful.

Think of the moving average line as a river. When the stock price is floating above the river, everything is flowing smoothly. When the price drops below the river, it's like falling in - things can get rough quickly.

A Real Example

Moving Average Settings

Pull up Apple's daily chart on TradingView and add the 50-day MA (click "Indicators" at the top, search "EMA," and add "Moving Average Exponential" with a length of 50). Click on settings You'll see a smooth line weaving through the candlesticks.

Look at periods where Apple's price stayed above the 50-day line for weeks. Those are the uptrends we identified in Chapter 6. Now look at moments where the price crashed below the line. Those are the danger zones where sellers took over. The moving average didn't predict those drops, but it confirmed the shift in momentum the moment it happened.

Gamer Translation: The Moving Average is your compass. Price above the line = heading north (bullish). Price below the line = heading south (bearish). Don't fight the direction of the compass.

Power-Up #2: Volume - The Crowd Meter

Volume is one of the most underrated tools in all of trading, and it's also one of the easiest to understand.

Volume measures how many shares of a stock were traded during a given time period. It shows up as bars at the bottom of your chart - tall bars mean lots of shares changed hands, short bars mean relatively few.

Think of volume as a crowd meter at a concert. If thousands of people are showing up, the event is real. If the venue is almost empty, something's off.

Why Volume Matters

Volume

Volume tells you how much conviction is behind a price move. And that makes a massive difference.

High volume + price going up = strong move. Lots of buyers are piling in with real money. The rally has conviction. Think of it as an army charging forward with full force.

Low volume + price going up = weak move. The price is rising, but not many people are participating. It's like a fake push - a bluff with no backup. These rallies often fizzle out.

High volume + price going down = serious selling. A lot of people are exiting at once. The drop is real and could continue. This is when you want your stop-loss ready.

Low volume + price going down = light pullback. The price is dipping, but sellers aren't very aggressive. It's probably a normal, healthy dip in an uptrend - not a reason to panic.

How to Add Volume on TradingView

Volume is usually on by default in TradingView, shown as bars at the very bottom of your chart. If you don't see it, click "Indicators," search for "Volume," and add it. The bars are colored green (more buying) and red (more selling) to match the candlesticks above them.

Make a habit of glancing at the volume bars every time you look at a chart. Before long, you'll instinctively notice when a move has real volume behind it and when it doesn't.

Gamer Translation: Volume is the crowd meter. High volume = packed arena, the action is real. Low volume = empty server, don't trust the move. Always check whether the crowd showed up before you commit to a trade.

Power-Up #3: RSI - The Energy Bar

Every character in every game has a stamina or energy bar. When it's full, the character can sprint, attack, and dodge. When it's drained, the character slows down, becomes vulnerable, and needs to rest before going again.

The **RSI (Relative Strength Index)** is a stock's energy bar. It measures how fast and how far a stock's price has moved recently, and it tells you whether the stock is running out of energy or still has plenty of fuel.

How It Works

Relative Strength Index

RSI is displayed as a number between 0 and 100, shown in its own panel below the main chart. It calculates the average gains versus the average losses over the past 14 days (the default setting) and plots the result.

There are two key zones:

RSI above 70 = Overbought. The stock has been running hard and fast. Its energy bar is nearly drained. This doesn't mean the price will crash immediately, but it warns you that the stock is exhausted and a pullback is increasingly likely. Buying here is risky - you're getting in when the character is already gasping for breath.

RSI below 30 = Oversold. The stock has been beaten down aggressively. Its energy bar has been depleted by heavy selling. This signals that sellers might be running out of steam and a bounce could be coming. It's like a character that's been knocked down but is about to get a second wind.

RSI between 30 and 70 = Neutral zone. The stock has normal energy levels. Neither overextended in either direction. Most of the time, RSI hangs out in this middle zone, and that's perfectly fine.

A Real Example

In January 2023, Tesla's RSI dropped below 30 after weeks of heavy selling. The stock had fallen from around $125 to below $110, and the RSI was flashing "oversold." For traders watching the energy bar, this was a signal that the selling pressure was exhausted. Within weeks, Tesla bounced and rallied back above $190.

On the other side, when NVIDIA surged past $500 in late 2023 on AI hype, its RSI climbed above 80. The stock was running incredibly hot. Traders watching the energy bar knew that a pullback was likely at some point. Sure enough, NVIDIA pulled back about 10% before resuming its climb.

Notice something important: the RSI didn't tell traders *when exactly* the reversal would happen. It just said, "Energy is running low - be careful." That's the right way to use it. It's a warning light, not a stop sign.

How to Add RSI on TradingView

Click "Indicators" at the top of TradingView, search for "RSI," and add "Relative Strength Index." It will appear in a panel below your chart with a line that oscillates between 0 and 100. You'll see horizontal lines at 70 and 30 marking the overbought and oversold zones.

Gamer Translation: RSI is the energy bar. Above 70 = exhausted, might need to rest. Below 30 = beaten down, might be ready to bounce. Between 30 and 70 = normal energy. Never buy a stock with a drained energy bar unless you know exactly what you're doing.

Using Your Power-Ups Together - The Confirmation Stack

Each indicator is useful on its own. But the real magic happens when you combine them. When multiple tools point in the same direction, your confidence in a trade goes way up. Traders call this **confirmation** - one tool backs up what another is telling you.

Here's how the three power-ups work as a team:

Confirming a Buy with MA + Volume

You're watching Amazon on the daily chart. The price has been above the 50-day Moving Average for three weeks - the compass says "bullish." The stock pulls back for a few days on low volume - the crowd meter says this is just a light dip, not serious selling. Then the price bounces and a green candle appears with **above-average volume**. The crowd is back.

That's a confirmed setup: trend is up (MA), the dip was on weak volume (sellers weren't aggressive), and the bounce has conviction (volume surged). Two power-ups agree - it's a stronger signal than any single indicator alone. If you see more green volume bars and the stock price is above the 50-day EMA, that's a good sign to consider buying the stock.

Moving Average + Volume

Avoiding a Bad Trade with RSI

You're excited about NVIDIA because the price just shot up 8% in two days. Your gut says "Buy now before it goes higher!" But you check the RSI, and it's sitting at 78 - deep in overbought territory. The energy bar is nearly drained.

The RSI doesn't mean NVIDIA can't go higher. It can. But it tells you that the risk of a pullback is elevated. Instead of chasing the move, you decide to wait for the RSI to cool down below 70 before looking for an entry. You saved yourself from potentially buying at the top of a short-term spike.

That's the power of indicators: they don't just tell you when to act. They also tell you when *not* to act. And sometimes, the best trade is the one you didn't make.

NVDA RSI

Important Reminder: Indicators are tools, not crystal balls. They give you better information, but they can be wrong. Never rely on a single indicator to make a trade. Always combine them with support and resistance, trend identification, and your own common sense.

Case Study: Noah Uses All Three Power-Ups

Noah is 24 and lives in Dallas. He's been paper trading for three weeks and has gotten comfortable reading charts. Today he opens his watchlist and checks Microsoft (MSFT).

Here's what he sees:

Moving Average: Microsoft's price is sitting above the 50-day MA. The compass says bullish.

Price action: The stock pulled back to a support level he drew last week at $405. It bounced with a strong green candle today.

Volume: Today's bounce came with volume well above the 20-day average. The crowd showed up.

RSI: Currently at 44 - neutral zone. Plenty of energy. Not overbought at all.

Noah counts the signals. Trend is up (MA). Price bounced off support (Chapter 7 skill). Volume confirms the bounce is real. RSI says there's room to run. All four indicators point in the same direction.

He places a paper trade: buys 25 shares of Microsoft at $407. He sets his stop-loss at $399 (just below support). His target is $425, near the next resistance level. If he's wrong, he loses about $8 per share. If he's right, he gains about $18 per share. That's a risk-reward ratio of roughly 1:2 - meaning the potential reward is double the potential risk.

Over the next week, Microsoft climbs to $421. Noah doesn't hit his full target yet, but he's sitting on a healthy gain and his stop-loss has protected his downside every step of the way. More importantly, he made the trade based on a system, not a feeling. Informed and skilled trading warrior on the rise.

Level 8 Complete - Three Power-Ups Equipped

Your HUD just got a serious upgrade. You now have three tools that professional traders use every single day. Let's lock them in:

Moving Average = your trend compass. Price above the 50-day MA means the trend is up. Price below means caution. Trade in the direction the compass points.

Volume = your crowd meter. High volume confirms real moves. Low volume warns of fake ones. Always check whether the crowd showed up.

RSI = your energy bar. Above 70 means overbought - the stock might need rest. Below 30 means oversold - a bounce could be brewing. Use it to avoid chasing and to spot potential opportunities.

Combine them for confirmation. One indicator is a hint. Two indicators agreeing is a signal. Three is a strong setup. Never rely on just one.

Chapter 8 Mission

Path A: The Journal

Step 1: Open TradingView and add three indicators to your chart: Moving Average (set to 50), Volume (usually on by default), and RSI. Do this for all five of your watchlist stocks.

Step 2: For each stock, answer three questions in your journal: Is the price above or below the 50-day MA? What did volume look like on the most recent big candle? Is the RSI above 70, below 30, or in the neutral zone?

Step 3: Find one stock where the Moving Average and Volume both confirm a bullish signal (price above MA, recent bounce on strong volume, RSI not overbought). Place a paper trade on it with a stop-loss below the nearest support level.

Step 4: Find one stock where the RSI is above 70. Write it down in your journal and add a note: "Overbought - wait for RSI to cool before considering a buy." This is you practicing the discipline of NOT trading, which is just as important as trading.

Mission time: 25 minutes. Difficulty: Medium-Hard. XP earned: You can now confirm trades using three professional-grade tools.

Path B: The Mission Log Dashboard

If you want structured indicator exercises, open the Paper Trading Boss Battles Mission Log Dashboard. Three missions across two chapters cover every indicator in this chapter:

Volume Check -Navigate to Chapter 4: Beginner Missions, open Chart Reading, and find exercise four. Find a stock that moved two percent or more, then analyse whether volume confirmed the move. Enter the ticker, the date, and your analysis of whether the volume spike validated the price action.

50-Day Moving Average -Exercise five in the same Chart Reading set. Check three stocks and note whether each is trading above or below the 50-day MA, then identify the pattern. Two out of three above suggests a bullish market. These two exercises plus the three from earlier chapters make up the full Chart Reading mission (+250 XP). Complete four of five to earn it.

RSI Analysis (+200 XP)-Navigate to Chapter 6: Strategy Mode and open Advanced Indicators. The first indicator is RSI. Enter the ticker, current reading, select whether it's oversold, neutral, or overbought, check for divergence, call your signal, and write your analysis. Complete three of the five indicators in this set to earn the XP.

~ ~ ~

Both paths teach the same lesson: never trade on price alone. The journal has you scan all five watchlist stocks with three indicators and make both a bullish trade and a disciplined pass. The dashboard breaks each indicator into its own exercise with structured fields and dropdowns. Either way, you now confirm every move with three power-ups.

Coming Up Next: Building Your Loadout

You now have an impressive toolkit. You can read candlestick charts, spot trends, identify support and resistance, and use three indicators to confirm your trades. Those are real skills that most adults never develop.

But skills without a plan are just tricks. No serious gamer enters a ranked match without a strategy. They pick their weapons, plan their rotations, and know their escape routes before the match even starts.

In Chapter 9, we're going to take everything you've learned and build it into your first complete trading plan - your personal **loadout**. You'll define your entry rules (when to buy), your exit rules (when to sell for profit), your stop-loss rules (when to cut losses), and how much virtual capital to put into each trade. By the end, you'll have a written plan that turns you from a casual trader into a disciplined one.

Your loadout is waiting. Let's build it.

Chapter 9

Building Your Loadout - Your First Trading Plan

No serious gamer enters a ranked match without a strategy.

You pick your weapons. You plan your rotations. You know your escape routes. You decide in advance what you'll do if you're ambushed, what you'll do if you get the high ground, and what you'll do if your teammate goes down. The plan doesn't guarantee a win, but it means you're never frozen in the moment, scrambling for a decision.

Esports professionals take this even further. They study opponent replays, drill specific scenarios, and enter every tournament with detailed game plans. The best players in the world aren't just talented - they're the most prepared.

A trading plan is your loadout for the stock market. It's a written set of rules that tells you exactly when to buy, when to sell, when to cut your losses, and how much money to put into each trade. Without it, you're guessing. With it, every decision is pre-made, logical, and repeatable.

In this chapter, you're going to build your first trading plan from scratch. Then you'll test it with three real paper trades. By the end, you'll have a written system that turns everything you've learned so far into a single, coherent strategy.

Let's build your loadout.

Why Every Trader Needs a Plan - Discipline Beats Talent

Here's something that surprises most beginners: the best traders in the world aren't the smartest people in the room. They're the most disciplined.

You can know everything about charts, indicators, and company earnings. But if you don't have a plan - a set of rules you follow every single time - your emotions will override your knowledge the moment real pressure hits. You'll buy because of FOMO. You'll hold a losing trade because of pride. You'll sell a winner too early because of fear.

Sound familiar? It's exactly like gaming. A talented player who tilts and makes emotional decisions will lose to a less-skilled player who stays calm and follows their game plan. In esports, in chess, and in trading, **discipline beats talent every time.** That is a big life lession my friend!

A trading plan is how you build that discipline. It takes the decision-making out of the heat of the moment and puts it on paper before you ever click "Buy." You're not deciding what to do when the stock drops 5% - you already decided that last Tuesday when you wrote your plan.

Professional traders at hedge funds and investment banks don't wing it. They follow systems. They have rules for every situation. And those rules are written down, tested, and followed without exception. Your trading plan is Version 1.0 of that same system.

Gamer Tip: An esports pro doesn't rethink their crosshair settings during a tournament match. They locked that in during practice. Your trading plan is the same idea - make the important decisions during calm planning time, not during the chaos of a live market.

The Four Components of Your Trading Plan

A complete trading plan answers four questions before you ever enter a trade. Miss any one of them, and you have a gap in your armor. Let's build each one.

Component 1: Entry Rules - When to Buy

Your entry rules define the exact conditions that must be true before you click "Buy." They prevent you from buying on impulse, chasing spikes, or entering a trade just because you're bored.

Using everything you've learned so far, here's a solid set of beginner entry rules:

Rule 1: The stock must be in an uptrend (Chapter 6). Price should be making higher highs and higher lows.

Rule 2: The stock's price must be above the 50-day Moving Average (Chapter 8). The compass must point bullish.

Rule 3: The stock should be near a support level (Chapter 7). You're buying near the floor, not the ceiling.

Rule 4: RSI should be below 70 (Chapter 8). You don't want to buy an exhausted stock.

Rule 5: The entry candle should have above-average volume (Chapter 8). The crowd must confirm the move.

If all five conditions are met, you buy. If even one is missing, you wait. No exceptions. That's how rules work.

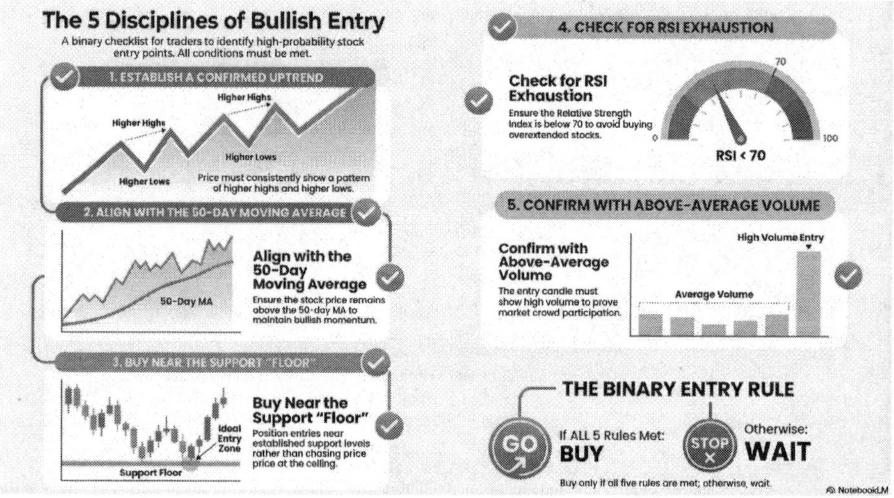

Entry Rules

Component 2: Exit Rules - When to Sell for Profit

This is where most beginners fall apart. They know when to get in, but they have no idea when to get out. They hold winners too long and watch profits evaporate, or they panic-sell a perfectly good trade the moment it dips a little.

Your exit rules define when to take your profit and walk away. Here are beginner-friendly options:

Target exit: Set a profit target before you enter the trade. For example: "I'll sell when the stock reaches the next resistance level." You identified resistance in Chapter 7. Use it.

Percentage exit: Decide in advance to sell when you're up a certain percentage. For example: "I'll take profit when the stock is up 8–10% from my entry."

Indicator exit: Sell when the RSI hits overbought territory (above 70) or when the price drops below the 50-day Moving Average.

Pick one method and write it down. You can experiment with different exit strategies over time, but starting with one clear rule is far better than having no rule at all.

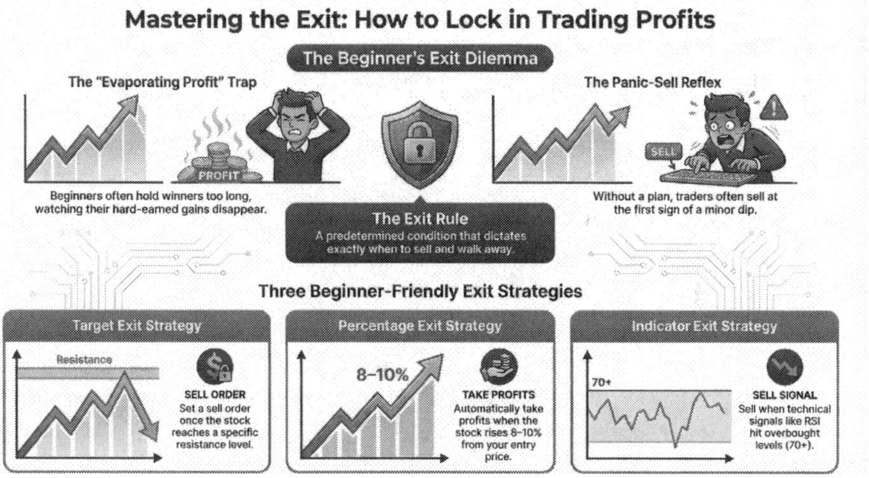

Exit Rules

Component 3: Stop-Loss Rules - When to Cut Your Losses

We've talked about stop-losses in almost every chapter so far, and for good reason. They are the single most important risk management tool in trading. Your stop-loss rule answers the question: *How much am I willing to lose on this trade before I get out?*

Here's a simple beginner stop-loss rule: **place your stop-loss just below the nearest support level.** If you bought a stock at $108 near a support level of $105, setting your stop-loss at $103 means you're risking $5 per share. If the support breaks, you're out before the damage gets worse.

Another approach is a **percentage-based stop-loss**. Some traders set a fixed rule like: "I will never lose more than 5–7% on a single trade." If you bought at $100, your stop-loss sits at $93–95.

The number doesn't matter as much as the rule. What matters is that you **always** have a stop-loss on every trade, and you **never** move it further away from your entry. Moving your stop-loss to avoid getting stopped out is like taking off your armor mid-battle. It defeats the whole purpose.

Stop-Loss Rules

Component 4: Position Sizing - How Much to Risk Per Trade

This is the component most beginners skip entirely, and it's the one that saves your account from disaster.

Position sizing means deciding how much of your total virtual capital to put into a single trade. The golden rule for beginners: **never risk more than 5% of your total account on a single trade.**

If your paper trading account has $100,000, that means the maximum amount you should be willing to lose on any one trade is $5,000. Not invest $5,000 - *lose* $5,000. That's an important distinction.

Here's a quick calculation. Say you want to buy a stock at $50 and your stop-loss is at $47. That's a $3 risk per share. If you're allowed to risk $5,000 total, you can buy a maximum of $5,000 ÷ $3 = 1,666 shares. In practice, you'd probably buy fewer to keep things simple, but the math keeps you from going all-in on any single trade.

Why does this matter? Because even the best traders lose on 40–50% of their trades. If you bet your entire account on one trade and it goes wrong, you're done. But if you risk only 5% per trade, you could lose ten trades in a row and still have half your capital left to keep going.

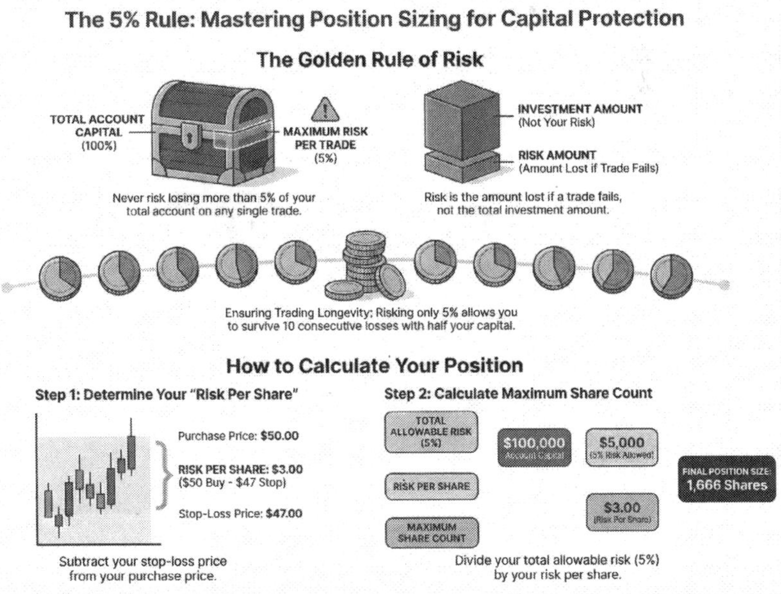

Position Sizing

Gamer Translation:

Entry rules = when to engage.

Exit rules = when to collect the loot and leave.

Stop-loss = your emergency eject.

Position sizing = never going all-in. A complete loadout covers all four.

Miss one and you're walking into a ranked match with a gap in your armor.

Your Trading Plan Template - Fill This In

Open your Paper Trading Journal to a fresh page. Write "My Trading Plan - Version 1.0" at the top. Then copy and fill in the following template. This is your playbook from now on.

My Entry Rules: I will only buy when: (list your conditions - trend, MA, support, RSI, volume)

My Exit Rules: I will take profit when: (choose your method - target price, percentage gain, or indicator signal)

My Stop-Loss Rules: I will exit a losing trade when: (below support, or fixed percentage like 5–7%)

My Position Sizing Rule: I will never risk more than ___% of my total account on a single trade.

My Watchlist: (list your five stocks from Chapter 4)

My Trading Schedule: I will check my charts at: (choose a consistent time - after school, in the evening)

This plan isn't set in stone. It's Version 1.0. As you learn more and gain experience, you'll refine it. But having a written plan - even a simple one - puts you ahead of the vast majority of people who try trading without any structure at all.

Case Study: Ava Writes Her Plan and Executes Three Trades

Ava is 18 and lives in Portland, Oregon. She's been paper trading for a month, and her results so far have been mixed - a couple of winners, a couple of losers, and no clear pattern. She realizes the problem: she's been trading on gut feeling. Time to build a real plan.

She opens her journal and writes her Version 1.0 plan:

Entry Rules: Stock in uptrend. Price above 50-day MA. Near support. RSI below 70. Volume above average on entry candle.

Exit Rules: Sell at the next resistance level or when up 8–10%.

Stop-Loss: Below the nearest support level. Maximum loss of 5% per trade.

Position Size: Risk no more than 5% of total account per trade.

Now she tests it with three trades over two weeks.

Trade 1 - Microsoft (MSFT): All five entry rules checked out. She bought 30 shares at $410 with a stop-loss at $398 and a target near resistance at $435. Eight days later, Microsoft hit $432. She sold and banked $22 per share. Win.

Trade 2 - Amazon (AMZN): Entry rules looked good: uptrend, above MA, near support, RSI at 52. She bought 20 shares at $178. Three days later, Amazon dropped on unexpected news about slower cloud growth. It hit her stop-loss at $170 and she was automatically sold out. She lost $8 per share. Loss - but a controlled, planned loss.

Trade 3 - Nike (NKE): She almost bought Nike because she saw a sharp green candle. But when she checked her rules, the stock was below its 50-day MA and the overall trend was still down. Her plan said don't buy. She skipped the trade. Two days later, Nike dropped another 4%. Her plan saved her from a bad trade.

After three trades, Ava has one win, one controlled loss, and one avoided mistake. More importantly, she made every decision based on her written plan, not her emotions. She writes in her journal: "The plan didn't make me feel anything. That's the point. It just told me what to do."

That's the shift. That's what separates traders from gamblers.

Level 9 Complete - Your Loadout Is Built

You now have something that most people who try trading never build: a written, rule-based trading plan. Let's lock in the essentials:

Discipline beats talent. The best traders follow systems. Your trading plan is your system. Writing it down transforms random trades into a repeatable process.

Four components, no gaps. Entry rules (when to buy), exit rules (when to sell for profit), stop-loss rules (when to cut losses), and position sizing (how much to risk). Miss any one and your plan has a hole in it.

Position sizing protects your account. Never risk more than 5% on a single trade. Even the best traders lose regularly - position sizing ensures one bad trade doesn't wipe you out.

The plan works even when it loses. Ava's Amazon trade lost money, but it was a good trade because she followed her rules and the loss was controlled. A planned loss is a successful process.

Chapter 9 Mission

Path A: The Journal

Step 1: In your Paper Trading Journal, write out your complete Trading Plan - Version 1.0. Use the template from this chapter. Be specific: list your exact entry conditions, your exit method, your stop-loss approach, and your position sizing rule.

Step 2: Scan your five watchlist stocks. Find one that currently meets all of your entry rules. If none qualify right now, that's fine - a plan also tells you when NOT to trade.

Step 3: Execute three paper trades over the next one to two weeks using your plan. For each trade, record everything in your journal: the stock, the date, your entry price, stop-loss level, profit target, position size, and which entry rules were checked.

Step 4: After all three trades are closed (win or lose), review each one. Did you follow your plan? Did any trade break a rule? Write down one lesson from each trade. These notes are the raw material for improving your Version 2.0.

Mission time: 30 minutes for the plan, plus 1–2 weeks for three trades. Difficulty: Hard. XP earned: You are now a rule-based, disciplined paper trader.

Path B: The Mission Log Dashboard

If you want your trading plan built, tested, and reviewed inside a structured system, open the Paper Trading Boss Battles Mission Log Dashboard. Four missions walk you through the full cycle:

Trading Rules (+200 XP)-Navigate to Chapter 1: Player Profile and open Trading Rules. Eight fill-in-the-blank rules form the core of your plan: max risk per trade, stop-loss method, minimum confluence signals, minimum risk-to-reward ratio, max trades per day, loss limit before stopping, routine compliance, and minimum confidence score. Fill in every blank to lock your rules.

Log Trades (+250 XP)-Navigate to Chapter 2: Trade Log and log your three paper trades. Each entry captures date, ticker, direction, strategy, entry and exit prices, shares, stop-loss, target, confluence count, emotional state, plan compliance, and a one-sentence lesson.

Replay Analysis (+200 XP)-After your trades close, open Replay Analysis in the same chapter. Eight review prompts ask for your win rate, best trade, worst trade, emotional patterns, strongest strategy, compliance count, biases spotted, and one skill to focus on next. Answer five or more to complete the mission.

Quick Reference Card (+100 XP)-A four-panel checklist covering Pre-Trade, During Trade, Post-Trade, and Weekly review steps. This is your plan condensed into a card you can glance at before every session.

~ ~ ~

Both paths follow the same arc: write the plan, trade the plan, review the plan. The journal keeps it in your own words. The dashboard gives you structured rules, a full trade log, an eight-prompt replay review, and a quick reference card. Version 1.0 is just the start.

Coming Up Next: Game Over? Nah.

You've built your plan and tested it. Some of your trades probably worked. And some probably didn't. That's completely normal.

But here's the part nobody talks about until it happens: losing stings. Even when it's virtual money. Even when you followed your plan perfectly. Even when you know logically that losses are part of the game. That first red trade hits different.

Every gamer has rage-quit at least once. But the ones who become legends? They watch the replay, figure out what went wrong, and come back better. Losing trades are your replays.

In Chapter 10, we're going to talk about the most important skill in all of trading: handling losses. You'll learn why losses are normal and necessary, how to build a trade journal that turns every loss into a lesson, and how to develop the mindset that keeps you in the game long after others have given up.

Game over? Nah. Not even close.

Chapter 10

Game Over? Nah. - Handling Losses and Learning from Mistakes

Every gamer has rage-quit at least once.

You know the feeling. You've been playing well, everything's going your way, and then one bad play turns into two, which turns into three, and suddenly you're slamming your controller on the desk and swearing you'll never play this stupid game again.

An hour later, you're back. Because deep down you know the game isn't the problem. You just had a bad run.

Trading losses feel exactly like that. You follow your plan. You check your indicators. You place a smart, well-reasoned trade. And then the stock drops, your stop-loss triggers, and you're staring at a red number in your portfolio. Even though it's virtual money, the sting is real.

This chapter is about that sting. We're going to talk honestly about losing - why it happens to everyone, why it's actually necessary, and how the best traders in the world turn losses into their greatest source of learning. The ones who become legends don't avoid losses. They watch the replay, figure out what went wrong, and come back better.

Game over? Not even close.

Why Losses Are Normal and Necessary

Here's a fact that shocks most beginners: **even the best traders in the world lose on 40–50% of their trades.**

Read that again. The professionals - people who manage billions of dollars at hedge funds, people who trade for a living, people who have been doing this for decades - are wrong about half the time. Some of the most successful traders in history have win rates of only 55% or even lower.

How is that possible? How can someone lose almost half their trades and still make money?

The answer is simple and powerful: **they make more on their winners than they lose on their losers.** If your average winning trade earns $300 and your average losing trade costs $150, you can lose half your trades and still come out ahead. The math works in your favor.

This is why stop-losses and position sizing matter so much. They keep your losses small and controlled. Your winners take care of the rest.

The Baseball Analogy

Think about baseball. The greatest hitters of all time - legends in the Hall of Fame - had batting averages around .300. That means they failed to get a hit 70% of the time. Seven out of every ten at-bats, they walked back to the dugout empty-handed.

Nobody called them failures. Nobody told them to quit. Because in baseball, you don't need to get a hit every time. You need to get hits when they count and make your hits bigger than your outs.

Trading is the exact same game. You will lose. Expect it. Accept it. Plan for it. And then focus on making your wins count.

Gamer Tip: In competitive games, nobody wins every single match. Even the top-ranked players have loss streaks. What separates them from everyone else is that they don't let losses destroy their confidence or change their strategy. They stick to the process.

Your Trade Journal - The Personal Replay System

In esports, every serious team reviews their matches after playing them. They sit down, watch the replay, and break down exactly what happened. What worked. What didn't. What they'll do differently next time.

Your **trade journal** is your replay system. It's the single most powerful learning tool you'll ever have as a trader - more valuable than any indicator, any book, or any YouTube video. Because it's built entirely from your own trades, your own decisions, and your own patterns.

What to Record After Every Trade

Every time you close a trade - win or lose - you record the following in your journal:

Date: When you entered and when you exited.

Stock: Which company and ticker symbol.

Entry price: What you paid per share.

Exit price: What you sold for.

Position size: How many shares you bought.

Stop-loss level: Where you set your emergency exit.

Result: Win or loss, and the dollar amount.

Setup quality: Did the trade meet all your entry rules from Chapter 9, or did you bend a rule?

Lesson learned: One sentence about what this trade taught you.

That last line - the lesson learned - is the most important. It forces you to think about every trade as a learning experience, not just a result. A trade that lost money but taught you to be more patient with your entries is worth more than a lucky win that taught you nothing.

The Ten-Trade Review

After every **ten trades**, stop and do a full review. Read through all ten entries and look for patterns:

How many wins? How many losses? What's your win rate so far?

What's your average win size versus your average loss size? Are your winners bigger than your losers?

Did any trades break your plan rules? What happened when you went off-plan?

Is there a pattern in your losses? Are they clustered in one sector, one time of day, or one type of setup?

This ten-trade review is where the real breakthroughs happen. You'll spot weaknesses you didn't know you had and strengths you didn't realize you'd developed. It's the difference between playing a hundred matches and never improving versus playing ten matches and learning from every single one.

Gamer Translation: Your trade journal is the match replay. Pros review every game. Amateurs just queue up the next match without thinking. Which one do you want to be? An amature or a Pro?

The Three Mistakes Every Beginner Makes - and How to Beat Them

After reviewing thousands of beginner trades, three mistakes show up again and again. They're so common that you will almost certainly make all three at some point. Knowing them in advance is like knowing where the traps are on a map. You might still step on one, but at least you'll recognize what happened.

Mistake #1: Revenge Trading

You lose a trade. It stings. Instead of stepping back and analyzing what happened, you immediately jump into another trade to "win the money back." You're not thinking clearly. You're trading angry.

This is **revenge trading**, and it's the fastest way to turn one loss into five. It's exactly like rage-queuing in a competitive game after a bad match. You're tilted, your judgment is clouded, and you make worse decisions than you normally would.

The fix: After a losing trade, close your trading platform. Walk away. Come back the next day with a clear head. Write your journal entry first. Then - and only then - look for a new setup. Never trade to get even. Trade because your plan says it's time.

Mistake #2: FOMO Buying

You see a stock shooting up 10% in a day. Your friends are talking about it. Social media is buzzing. Every fiber of your being screams "Buy now before it goes higher!"

So you buy. Right at the top. And within a day, the stock gives back half the gain and you're sitting on a loss.

This is **FOMO buying** - fear of missing out - and it's the single most expensive emotion in the stock market. FOMO makes you ignore your plan, skip your entry rules, and buy into hype instead of logic.

The fix: Every time you feel the urge to chase a hot stock, open your trading plan and check the entry rules. Does the trade meet every single condition? If not, you don't buy. Period. There will always be another opportunity. Always. The market opens again tomorrow.

Mistake #3: Ignoring Your Stop-Loss

You bought a stock at $50. Your stop-loss is at $47. The stock drops to $47.50 and you think, "It's so close to bouncing. I'll just move my stop-loss down to $44 to give it more room."

The stock drops to $44. You move it again to $40. Now you're down 20% and praying for a miracle. What started as a small, controlled loss turned into a devastating one - all because you moved your stop-loss.

This is the most dangerous mistake a trader can make. Your stop-loss is your armor. **Moving it further away to avoid getting stopped out is like taking off your helmet in the middle of a fight because it's uncomfortable.**

The fix: Set your stop-loss when you enter the trade. Then don't touch it. Let it do its job. If you get stopped out, accept the small loss, record it in your journal, and move on. A small loss is a tiny scratch. Ignoring your stop-loss is how small scratches become broken bones.

Remember: Revenge trading, FOMO buying, and ignoring stop-losses are the three bosses of beginner mistakes. You will face all three. But now you know their attack patterns, and you have the fixes loaded into your plan.

The Mindset Shift - "I Didn't Lose Money, I Paid Tuition"

This is the most important idea in this entire chapter, and maybe in this entire book.

Every losing trade teaches you something. Every single one. If you review it honestly and extract the lesson, that loss becomes an investment in your education. You didn't lose money - you paid tuition.

Think about every game you've ever gotten good at. You didn't start as an expert. You got destroyed over and over again. You lost to players who knew things you didn't. And each loss, if you paid attention, taught you something that made you better.

The only truly wasted loss is one you don't learn from. So learn from your mistakes and get better, gain sight into making a better plan. Become a Pro.

How to Analyze a Loss Without Emotion

After a losing trade, wait at least a few hours (ideally until the next day) before doing your analysis. This puts emotional distance between you and the result. Then ask yourself these four questions, like a chess player reviewing a lost game move by move:

1. Did I follow my trading plan? If yes, the loss was just bad luck or an unpredictable event. The process was right even though the outcome was wrong. No changes needed - just move on.

2. Did I break any of my entry rules? If you skipped a condition - maybe the RSI was overbought but you bought anyway - there's your lesson. Next time, no exceptions.

3. Was my stop-loss in the right place? Did you set it too tight and get stopped out by normal noise? Or was it well-placed and the stock genuinely broke through support? This helps you calibrate your stop-loss for future trades.

4. What would I do differently? Write one specific, actionable change. Not "I'll do better" - that's vague. Something like: "Next time I'll wait for volume confirmation before entering."

This four-question review turns every loss into a lesson. Over time, your journal will become a treasure chest of hard-won wisdom that no book, course, or YouTube video can replicate.

Case Study: Diego's Three Losses and What They Taught Him

Diego is 23 and lives in Miami. Over the past three weeks, he's placed eight paper trades. Five were winners. Three were losers. The losses bothered him, so he sat down with his journal and reviewed each one.

Loss #1 - Tesla (TSLA): Diego bought Tesla after seeing it spike 6% in one day. He felt the FOMO pull and jumped in without checking his entry rules. RSI was at 76 - overbought. Two days later, Tesla pulled back 5% and his stop-loss triggered. His review: "I broke Rule 4 - RSI was above 70. I chased the move. Lesson: never buy an overbought stock, no matter how exciting the move looks."

Loss #2 - Nike (NKE): Diego followed every entry rule. Nike was in an uptrend, above the 50-day MA, near support, with good volume and neutral RSI. He bought at $106 with a stop-loss at $101. Two days later, Nike reported earnings that missed expectations and the stock gapped down to $98, blowing through his stop-loss. His review: "I followed my plan perfectly. The loss was caused by an earnings surprise I couldn't predict. Lesson: check the earnings calendar before entering a trade. I didn't realize Nike was reporting this week."

Loss #3 - Coca-Cola (KO): Diego bought Coca-Cola near support at $58. It dropped to his stop-loss at $56.50. He got stopped out. Two days later, Coca-Cola bounced back to $60. He felt frustrated - his stop was too tight. His review: "The support zone was $57–$58, but I set my stop-loss inside the zone instead of below it. Lesson: set stop-losses below the support zone, not at the edge of it. Give the stock room to breathe."

Three losses. Three completely different causes. One was emotional (FOMO). One was uncontrollable (earnings surprise). One was a technical mistake (tight stop). And each one taught him something specific he could fix.

Diego added all three lessons to his trading plan as new rules. His Version 1.0 was already evolving into Version 1.1. That's not failure. That's growth.

Level 10 Complete - Losses Are XP Now

You've faced the hardest truth in trading and come through stronger. Let's lock in the essentials:

Losses are normal. Even the best traders lose 40–50% of the time. You don't need to win every trade - you need your winners to be bigger than your losers.

Your trade journal is your most valuable tool. Record every trade. Review every ten. The patterns you discover in your own data will teach you more than anything else.

Know the three beginner traps. Revenge trading (trading angry), FOMO buying (chasing hype), and ignoring stop-losses (removing your armor). Recognize them when they show up and use the fixes.

Every loss is tuition. Review losses with the four-question system: Did I follow my plan? Did I break a rule? Was my stop-loss right? What would I do differently? Extract the lesson and your plan gets better every time.

Chapter 10 Mission

Path A: The Journal

Step 1: Go back through every paper trade you've made so far. For any trade that's missing a journal entry, write one now. Include all the fields: date, stock, entry, exit, result, and lesson learned.

Step 2: Do your first Ten-Trade Review. If you have ten or more trades, analyze them using the questions from this chapter. If you have fewer than ten, do the review with what you have.

Step 3: Identify your most common mistake so far. Is it FOMO? Revenge trading? Tight stop-losses? Something else? Write it at the top of a new journal page as your "#1 Pattern to Fix."

Step 4: Update your trading plan. Based on your journal review, add at least one new rule or adjust an existing one. Write "Version 1.1" at the top. Your plan is alive and improving.

Mission time: 30 minutes. Difficulty: Hard (emotionally). XP earned: You now treat losses as data, not disasters.

Path B: The Mission Log Dashboard

If you want a structured review system that also builds your emotional playbook, open the Paper Trading Boss Battles Mission Log Dashboard. Four missions cover the full loss-and-learn cycle:

Boss Battle #1 (+300 XP)-Navigate to Chapter 4: Beginner Missions. This is a ten-trade scorecard. Log every trade with ticker, direction, entry, exit, stop, shares, P&L, whether you followed the plan, and the lesson learned. Eight or more trades completes the battle. This is your Ten-Trade Review in structured form.

Tilt Triggers (+150 XP)-Navigate to Chapter 3: Emotion Tracker. Four categories of triggers are listed: Loss, FOMO, External, and Market. Check every trigger that has affected you. Identifying three or more completes the mission. This is where you name your #1 Pattern to Fix.

Cooldown Protocol (+200 XP)-In the same chapter, build your five-step Cooldown Protocol: Recognize, Stop, Breathe, Reflect, Return. Each step has a text field where you write your personal version-what your body feels when you're tilted, what you'll do to step away, how you'll breathe, what question you'll ask yourself, and what state you need before returning to trade.

Replay Analysis (+200 XP)-Navigate to Chapter 2: Trade Log. Eight prompts review your win rate, best trade, worst trade, emotional patterns, strategy performance, compliance, biases, and focus area. This is your Version 1.1 fuel-answer five or more to complete it.

~ ~ ~

Both paths turn losses into lessons. The journal has you backfill missing entries, run a ten-trade review, name your biggest mistake, and update your plan. The dashboard gives you a ten-trade scorecard, a tilt trigger checklist, a five-step cooldown protocol, and an eight-prompt replay analysis. Either way, your plan evolves to Version 1.1.

Coming Up Next: Boss Battle #1

You've learned the controls. You've explored the map. You've unlocked power-ups and built your loadout. You've even learned how to take a hit and keep going.

There's only one thing left to do: prove it all works.

In Chapter 11, you're facing your first Boss Battle - a structured ten-trade challenge that tests everything you've learned across this entire book. You'll follow your trading plan, use your indicators, manage your risk, record every trade in your journal, and grade yourself honestly at the end.

This isn't a quiz. There are no right or wrong answers. It's a performance test - a chance to see exactly where you stand as a paper trader and what skills you'll carry into Book 2.

The Boss is waiting. You're ready!

Chapter 11

Boss Battle #1 - The Paper Trading Challenge

You've learned the controls, explored the map, unlocked power-ups, and built your loadout. Now it's time for your first Boss Battle.

Every great game builds toward a boss fight. You spend hours learning mechanics, collecting gear, and practising combos. And then the game drops you into an arena, the music changes, and a health bar appears at the top of the screen. Everything you've learned gets tested at once.

This chapter is your Boss Battle. in the arena of Paper Trading.

The Paper Trading Challenge is a structured ten-trade mission that tests every skill from this book: chart reading, support and resistance, indicators, your trading plan, risk management, journaling, and emotional discipline. It's not a quiz with right and wrong answers. It's a performance test - a real simulation that shows you exactly where your skills stand and where you need to level up.

When you finish, you'll have a clear, data-backed picture of yourself as a trader. Not what you hope you are. Not what you feel like you are. What your actual results say you are.

The Boss is waiting. Let's go!

The Ten-Trade Boss Battle - Rules and Scoring

This challenge runs over two to three weeks. You'll place exactly ten paper trades on U.S. stocks, following your trading plan from Chapter 9. Every trade gets recorded in your journal. That's 10 complete trades to buy and sell a stocks. At the end, you'll grade yourself on five categories. So let's get started!

Here are the rules:

Rule 1: Ten Trades, No More, No Less

You must complete exactly ten trades. Not eight because you ran out of motivation. Not fifteen because you got excited. Ten. This forces you to be selective about your entries and thoughtful about your timing. Quality over quantity - always.

Rule 2: Every Trade Must Follow Your Plan

Before you enter any trade, run through your entry checklist from Chapter 9. If all conditions are met, you trade. If even one condition is missing, you skip it and wait for a better setup. No exceptions. No "just this once." If you break your rules, you still record the trade, but you mark it as "Off-Plan" in your journal.

Rule 3: Every Trade Must Have a Stop-Loss

No trade enters the battlefield without a stop-loss in place. You decide your exit-for-loss before you click "Buy." If a trade doesn't have a stop-loss, it doesn't count.

Rule 4: Journal Everything

Every trade gets a full journal entry using the format from Chapter 10: date, stock, entry price, exit price, position size, stop-loss level, result, setup quality, and lesson learned. No shortcuts.

Rule 5: Honest Self-Evaluation

At the end of all ten trades, you grade yourself honestly. Not generously, not harshly - honestly. The goal isn't to look good. The goal is to know exactly where you stand and how you handled it.

Gamer Tip: A Boss Battle isn't designed to be easy. It's designed to test you. Some trades will win. Some will lose. That's expected. What matters is HOW you traded, not just what happened.

The Pre-Trade Checklist - Your Pre-Fight Ritual

Before every single trade in the challenge, run through this checklist. Print it out, tape it next to your screen, or copy it into the front page of your journal. It should become as automatic as checking your loadout before a match.

1. **Is the stock in an uptrend?** Check the daily chart. Are you seeing higher highs and higher lows? If the trend is down or unclear, stop here.
2. **Is the price above the 50-day Moving Average?** If the compass points bearish, don't fight it.
3. **Is the stock near a support level?** Are you buying near the floor, not the ceiling? Check your horizontal lines.
4. **Is RSI below 70?** If the energy bar is drained, the stock might pull back before it goes higher. Wait for a better entry.
5. **Is volume confirming the move?** Check whether the entry candle has above-average volume. Did the crowd show up?
6. **Have I set my stop-loss?** Know exactly where you'll exit for a loss before you enter. Write it down.
7. **Do I know my profit target?** Where will you take profit? The next resistance level? A percentage gain? Decide now.
8. **Is my position size within my rules?** Are you risking no more than 5% of your total account on this single trade?

If all eight boxes are checked, enter the trade. If any box is unchecked, walk away. The checklist is your armor inspection. Never skip it.

Gamer Translation: This checklist is your pre-match warmup. Esports pros don't skip warmups before tournament matches. You don't skip the checklist before trades. Build the habit now and it'll serve you for years.

Tracking Your Results - The Boss Battle Scorecard

After all ten trades are complete, it's time to pull out your journal and crunch some numbers. This is where paper trading transforms from a casual activity into a serious skill-building exercise.

Ready? Let's evaluate!

Path A: The Journal

Metric 1: Win Rate

How many of your ten trades were winners, and how many were losers? Divide your wins by ten and multiply by 100 to get your win percentage.

If you won six out of ten, your win rate is 60%. If you won four, it's 40%. Remember from Chapter 10 - even professional traders win only 50–60% of the time. *Don't beat yourself up if your number is below 50%. Focus on whether your winners were bigger than your losers.*

Metric 2: Average Gain vs. Average Loss

Add up the profit from all your winning trades and divide by the number of wins. That's your average gain. Do the same for your losses - add up all the losses and divide by the number of losing trades. That's your average loss.

The magic question: **is your average gain bigger than your average loss?** If you're averaging $250 per win and only $120 per loss, you're in great shape even with a 50% win rate. *If your average loss is bigger than your average gain, your stop-losses might need tightening or your profit targets need extending.*

Metric 3: Biggest Win and Biggest Loss

Find your single best trade and your single worst trade. How do they compare? In a healthy trading approach, your biggest win should be significantly larger than your biggest loss. *If your worst loss dwarfs your best win, that's a red flag that risk management needs work.*

Metric 4: Plan Compliance

Look through all ten journal entries. How many trades were fully "On-Plan" (every entry rule checked, stop-loss set, position sized correctly) versus "Off-Plan" (at least one rule broken)?

This might be the most important metric of all. A trader with a 40% win rate but 100% plan compliance is in a far better position than a trader with a 60% win rate who got lucky while ignoring their rules. *Luck runs out. Discipline doesn't.*

Metric 5: Biggest Lesson

Read through the "lesson learned" from all ten trades. Which lesson stands out as the most important? *Write it in large letters on a fresh journal page. That lesson is your single biggest takeaway from Beginner Mode - the one insight that will carry you into Book 2.*

Path B: The Mission Log Dashboard

If you want every metric calculated in structured fields, open the Paper Trading Boss Battles Mission Log Dashboard. Three missions capture all five metrics and more:

Monthly Stats (+200 XP)-Navigate to Chapter 8: Monthly Review and open Monthly Stats. Seventeen fields capture everything this chapter asks for and more. Enter your total trades, winners, losers, and the dashboard walks you through win rate, total dollars gained, total dollars lost, net P&L, average win, average loss, actual risk-to-reward ratio, biggest single win, biggest single loss, plan compliance percentage, sectors traded, average hold time, and your best and worst strategy. Every metric from this chapter has a dedicated field. This is your ten-trade review in one structured panel.

Best & Worst Analysis (+200 XP)-In the same chapter, open Best & Worst Analysis. Two detailed panels-one for your best trade, one for your worst-ask for the ticker, setup type, entry and exit details, and then the critical questions. For the winner: why did it work, and is it repeatable? For the loser: why did it fail, and what rule prevents it next time? This is Metric 3 and Metric 5 combined into a deep-dive exercise.

Replay Analysis (+200 XP)-Navigate to Chapter 2: Trade Log. Eight review prompts ask for your win rate, best trade, worst trade, emotional patterns, strongest strategy, compliance count, biases spotted, and the one skill to focus on next. Answer five or more to complete. Between Monthly Stats, Best & Worst, and Replay Analysis, every metric from this chapter is covered-plus emotional and strategy insights the journal version doesn't reach.

~ ~ ~

Both paths turn raw trades into real data. The journal has you calculate five metrics by hand-win rate, average gain versus average loss, biggest win and loss, plan compliance, and your biggest lesson. The dashboard gives you seventeen structured fields for those same metrics, a dedicated best-and-worst deep dive, and an eight-prompt replay review. One is manual, one is guided-both transform your ten trades from a pile of paper into a performance report.

Your Player Rating - Honest Self-Evaluation

Now grade yourself. Be honest. This isn't for anyone else - it's for you.

Rate yourself on each of the following skills from 1 to 5 (1 = just started learning, 3 = comfortable but still practicing, 5 = confident and consistent):

Chart Reading: Can you open a chart, identify the trend, and spot support and resistance?

Indicator Use: Can you read the Moving Average, Volume, and RSI and use them to confirm your trades?

Trade Planning: Do you enter every trade with a clear plan for entry, exit, and stop-loss?

Risk Management: Do you consistently use stop-losses and keep your position sizes within your rules?

Emotional Discipline: Can you handle losses without revenge trading, avoid FOMO, and stick to your plan under pressure?

Journaling: Do you record every trade and review your results regularly?

Add up your scores. The maximum is 30.

Your Score Card:

25–30: Elite Beginner. You've built strong foundations. You're ready for Book 2 with confidence.

18–24: Solid Progress. You've got the core skills but some areas need more practice. Consider running a second set of ten trades before moving on.

12–17: Still Building. You've learned a lot, but several skills need more reps. Re-read the chapters tied to your lowest scores and run another Boss Battle.

Below 12: Replay the Tutorial. No shame at all. Go back to Chapter 6, re-do the missions, and build up your reps. This game rewards patience.

Whatever your score, write it down with today's date. This is your baseline. When you finish Book 2 and take Boss Battle #2, you'll look back at this number and see exactly how far you've come.

Gamer Tip: Your player rating isn't a judgment. It's a snapshot. The best players in any game started at level one. What matters is that you're playing, you're tracking, and you're improving. That puts you ahead of 99% of people who only talk about learning the stock market. You are doing it, keep it going. The goal of this author is to build a whole generation of gamer guild who take life by the horns.

Case Study: Lily's Boss Battle Results

Lily is 24 and lives in Charlotte, North Carolina. She completed her ten-trade Boss Battle over three weeks. Here's her scorecard:

Win Rate: 5 wins, 5 losses - 50%. Right in line with professional averages.

Average Gain: $285 per winning trade. **Average Loss:** $145 per losing trade. Her winners were nearly double her losers. Even with a 50% win rate, she came out well ahead overall.

Biggest Win: $480 on a Microsoft trade that hit her resistance target perfectly. **Biggest Loss:** $210 on an Amazon trade that gapped down on unexpected news. Her biggest win was more than double her biggest loss. Good sign.

Plan Compliance: 8 out of 10 trades were fully On-Plan. Two trades broke rules - one was a FOMO buy on Tesla (she didn't check RSI, which was at 74), and one was a trade where she forgot to set her stop-loss until after she'd already entered.

Biggest Lesson: "The trades where I followed my plan felt calm and controlled, even when they lost. The two trades where I broke rules felt chaotic, even when one of them accidentally won. The plan isn't just about making money - it's about staying in control."

Player Rating: Chart Reading: 4. Indicators: 3. Planning: 4. Risk Management: 3. Emotional Discipline: 3. Journaling: 4. Total: 21 out of 30 - Solid Progress.

Lily wrote her score and the date in her journal. She circled Risk Management and Emotional Discipline as the two areas she'd focus on improving in Book 2. She didn't feel like she'd failed. She felt like she'd just completed the hardest level of a game and unlocked a clear map of exactly what to work on next.

That's what the Boss Battle is for.

Level Up - You've Beaten Beginner Mode

Take a breath. Look at what you've accomplished.

Eleven chapters ago, you didn't know what a stock was. You didn't know the difference between the NYSE and NASDAQ. You'd never seen a candlestick chart. The words "support," "resistance," and "RSI" meant nothing to you.

Now look at you.

You understand how the stock market works and why it moves. You can read candlestick charts across multiple timeframes. You can spot trends, identify support and resistance zones, and use three professional-grade indicators to confirm your analysis. You've built a written trading plan with rules for entry, exit, stop-loss, and position sizing. You've placed real paper trades on real U.S. stocks. You've handled losses, kept a trade journal, and graded yourself honestly.

You have skills that most adults never develop. You have a framework for thinking about money, risk, and strategy that will serve you for the rest of your life. And you did all of it without risking a single real dollar.

Beginner Mode: Complete.

The Path Ahead - Welcome to the Skill Tree

Beating Beginner Mode doesn't mean the game is over. It means the real game is just beginning.

In **Book 2: Paper Trading Boss Battles - The Trading Skill Tree**, we're going deeper. You'll learn to read company financial reports like a character stats sheet. You'll understand how the broader economy - GDP, inflation, Federal Reserve decisions - affects your trades. You'll do deep dives into individual market sectors, master risk management with professional-grade position sizing, discover your personal trading style, and learn to time your entries and exits with precision.

Book 2 is where you stop being a beginner and start building a real, comprehensive trading skill set. Every chapter unlocks a new branch on your skill tree, and the Boss Battle at the end is a full thirty-day trading campaign.

But for now, close your journal. Put down this book. And take a moment to appreciate what you've done.

You entered the arena as a curious player. You're leaving as a trained paper trader with real tools, real skills, and real experience. That's not nothing. That's everything.

Beginner Mode - Cleared.

Player Status - Ready for the Skill Tree.

See you in Book 2.

Save Point Reached - Your Game Has Just Begun

What You Now Carry

You started this book as a curious player loading into an unfamiliar game. Eleven chapters later, you're walking out of Beginner Mode with a skill set that most adults never build. Before we look ahead, let's be clear about what you now carry in your inventory - because it's more than you might realize.

You understand the arena. The stock market isn't a mysterious black box anymore. It's a skill-based system where real companies are bought and sold every day, driven by forces you can identify and analyze. Supply and demand, earnings reports, Federal Reserve decisions, institutional money flows - you know the game engine now. That knowledge doesn't expire.

You can read the battlefield. Charts, candlesticks, trends, support zones, resistance levels - these aren't abstract concepts to you anymore. They're tools you've used with your own hands on real U.S. stocks. You can open any chart in the world and within minutes identify whether buyers or sellers are in control. That's a skill most people twice your age don't have.

You trade with a system, not a feeling. You built a written trading plan with rules for entry, exit, stop-losses, and position sizing. You know the difference between a disciplined trade and a gamble. That distinction - system over impulse - is the single biggest separator between people who build wealth and people who lose it.

You know how to lose. That sounds strange, but it might be the most valuable thing in this entire book. You understand that losses are normal, that even professionals lose 40–50% of the time, and that a controlled loss recorded in a journal is worth more than a lucky win you can't repeat. You don't rage-quit. You review the replay.

You measure yourself honestly. Your Boss Battle scorecard gave you a real, data-backed picture of your strengths and weaknesses. No guessing. No inflated confidence. Just clear numbers that show you exactly where to focus next. That habit of honest self-assessment will serve you in trading, in school, in careers, and in life.

Where This Takes You

Right now, you're a paper trader. But the skills you've built don't stop at virtual money.

The teenagers who learn to read charts, manage risk, and follow a plan at thirteen don't just become good traders. They become better decision-makers in everything. They think about risk versus reward before making choices. They recognize when emotions are hijacking their judgment. They understand that patience and discipline beat talent and luck over any meaningful stretch of time.

Five years from now, when your friends are opening their first brokerage accounts with zero experience and learning the hard way, you'll already have hundreds of paper trades logged, a refined trading plan, and years of pattern recognition built into your brain. You won't be starting from scratch. You'll be continuing a journey you began right here.

Ten years from now, the compound effect of starting early - not just with money, but with knowledge - will be enormous. You'll look back at this book the way a professional athlete looks back at their first practice. Humble beginnings. But the beginning of everything.

The Obstacles Ahead - and How to Beat Them

Let's be honest about what's coming. Finishing this book is not the end of the challenge. It's the end of the tutorial. The real game starts now, and it comes with real obstacles.

You'll lose motivation. There will be weeks where you don't feel like checking your charts or updating your journal. That's normal. The fix isn't willpower - it's routine. Set a specific time each day, even just ten minutes after school, to scan your watchlist. Small, consistent habits beat occasional bursts of energy every time.

You'll feel like you're not improving. Progress in trading is slow and uneven. You'll have great weeks and terrible weeks. The journal is your proof that you're getting better, even when it doesn't feel like it. Trust the data over the feeling.

People won't understand what you're doing. Your friends might think paper trading is pointless because it's not real money. Some adults might not take it seriously. Ignore the noise. Every professional started by practicing before the stakes were real. Pilots use simulators. Athletes use scrimmages. Surgeons use cadaver labs. You use paper trading. The method is proven.

You'll be tempted to skip ahead to real money. Resist that urge. Paper trading is where you make your mistakes for free. Every bad habit you catch now is a lesson that would cost real dollars later. Stay in practice mode until your journal proves you're consistently following your plan and your wins are larger than your losses. The real market isn't going anywhere. It'll be there when you're ready.

Your Next Moves

Beginner Mode is complete, but the skill tree is wide open. Here's how to keep leveling up:

Keep trading. Run another ten-trade Boss Battle. Then another. Each round sharpens your skills and fills your journal with data you can't get any other way.

Upgrade your plan. Your Version 1.0 trading plan is a starting point. Every ten-trade review should produce at least one refinement. By the time you reach Version 3.0 or 4.0, your plan will be uniquely yours - shaped by your own strengths, weaknesses, and trading style.

Start Book 2. Paper Trading Boss Battles - The Trading Skill Tree takes everything from Beginner Mode and builds on it. You'll learn to analyze company financials, understand how the economy affects your trades, explore individual market sectors in depth, and develop a personal trading style. The Boss Battle at the end is a full thirty-day campaign.

Teach someone. The fastest way to lock in what you've learned is to explain it to someone else. Show a friend how to read a candlestick chart. Walk a sibling through what support and resistance mean. Teaching forces you to understand at a deeper level than reading ever will.

One Last Thing

Most people will never do what you just did. Most people will never pick up a book about the stock market at your age. Most people will never place a paper trade, keep a journal, build a plan, or face a Boss Battle. Most people will wait until they're thirty, forty, or older - and wish they'd started sooner.

You didn't wait.

You showed up. You learned the controls. You explored the map. You built your loadout. You took hits and kept going. And you walked out of Beginner Mode with skills, knowledge, and a journal full of proof that you did the work.

That's not nothing. That's everything.

The market opens again tomorrow. Your charts are waiting. Your plan is written. Your journal has blank pages ready to be filled.

Player One - save point reached. The adventure continues.

ENDNOTES

All stock prices, market capitalizations, and financial figures referenced in this book are approximate and were accurate as of 2025. Current values may differ. Readers should verify all financial data independently, as market conditions change continuously.

1. Warren Buffett purchased his first stock at the age of eleven. - Alice Schroeder, The Snowball: Warren Buffett and the Business of Life (New York: Bantam Books, 2008).

2. Buffett has stated publicly that his only regret was not starting sooner. - Berkshire Hathaway Annual Shareholder Letters; CNBC interview transcripts, various years.

3. The average American does not invest until the age of thirty-three. - Charles Schwab Modern Wealth Survey, 2023.

4. The power of compound growth means a dollar invested at thirteen can be worth significantly more than a dollar invested at thirty. - Based on S&P 500 historical average annual returns of approximately 10%. Data sourced from NYU Stern School of Business, Damodaran Online, "Historical Returns on Stocks, Bonds and Bills: 1928–2024."

5. Microsoft acquired Mojang Studios, the creator of Minecraft, in 2014 for $2.5 billion. - Microsoft Press Release, "Microsoft to Acquire Mojang," September 15, 2014.

6. The New York Stock Exchange has been operating since 1792 and is the oldest and largest stock exchange in the world. - NYSE official history, nyse.com; World Federation of Exchanges market data.

7. The Dow Jones Industrial Average tracks 30 of the largest U.S. companies. The S&P 500 tracks 500 of the largest publicly traded companies in the United States. - S&P Dow Jones Indices, factsheets available at spglobal.com.

8. The S&P 500 has returned roughly 10% per year on average over long periods. - NYU Stern School of Business, Damodaran Online, "Historical Returns on Stocks, Bonds and Bills: 1928–2024."

9. $1,000 invested at 10% annual growth becomes approximately $2,600 after 10 years, $6,700 after 20 years, and $17,400 after 30 years. - Standard compound interest formula: FV = PV × (1 + r)^n. These figures assume reinvested returns with no additional contributions.

10. Warren Buffett's net worth exceeds $145 billion. - Forbes Real-Time Billionaires List, forbes.com.

11. The Pattern Day Trader rule requires a minimum of $25,000 in a brokerage account to day trade freely. - FINRA Rule 4210; U.S. Securities and Exchange Commission, "Day Trading: Your Dollars at Risk," sec.gov.

12. U.S. stock market trading hours are 9:30 AM to 4:00 PM Eastern Time, Monday through Friday. - NYSE and NASDAQ official trading schedules.

13. Rivian held its Initial Public Offering in November 2021 and was briefly valued higher than Ford Motor Company. - Reuters, "Rivian Shares Surge in Debut," November 10, 2021; Bloomberg market data.

14. Ford Motor Company was founded in 1903 and has been manufacturing automobiles for over a century. - Ford Motor Company corporate history, corporate.ford.com.

15. Coca-Cola has paid consecutive quarterly dividends for over 60 years. - The Coca-Cola Company Investor Relations, dividend history, coca-colacompany.com.

16. Microsoft's market capitalization is approximately $3 trillion, based on a stock price near $400 and roughly 7.3 billion shares outstanding. - Yahoo Finance and Microsoft Investor Relations.

17. Market capitalization categories: large-cap ($10 billion and above), mid-cap ($2 billion to $10 billion), and small-cap (under $2 billion). - U.S. Securities and Exchange Commission, Investor.gov; Investopedia financial definitions.

18. The United States experienced one of the longest bull markets in history from 2009 to 2020. $1,000 invested in the S&P 500 at the start would have grown to roughly $5,000. - S&P 500 historical price data. Bull market began March 9, 2009. Total return calculation based on S&P 500 index performance.

19. A bear market is officially defined as a decline of 20% or more from recent highs. - U.S. Securities and Exchange Commission; standard financial industry definition.

20. During the COVID-19 pandemic, the S&P 500 fell over 30% in approximately five weeks in early 2020, then recovered to new all-time highs by August 2020. - S&P 500 historical data: peak February 19, 2020 to trough March 23, 2020 (approximately 34% decline). Recovery to new highs confirmed August 2020.

21. The Dow Jones Industrial Average has been in existence since 1896. - S&P Dow Jones Indices, official history.

22. The S&P 500 covers approximately 80% of the total value of the American stock market. - S&P Dow Jones Indices, S&P 500 factsheet, spglobal.com.

23. Investopedia Stock Simulator provides $100,000 in virtual cash for paper trading. - Investopedia.com, Stock Simulator feature page.

24. TradingView paper trading provides $100,000 in virtual cash. - TradingView.com, paper trading feature documentation.

25. Webull paper trading provides $1,000,000 in virtual cash. - Webull.com, paper trading feature page.

26. Thinkorswim paperMoney by Charles Schwab provides $100,000 in virtual cash. - Charles Schwab/Thinkorswim, paperMoney feature documentation.

27. Peter Lynch managed the Magellan Fund at Fidelity Investments from 1977 to 1990, achieving an average annual return of approximately 29%. - Peter Lynch, One Up on Wall Street (New York: Simon & Schuster, 1989); Fidelity Investments historical records. Widely cited as 29.2% annualized.

28. The Magellan Fund under Lynch became the best-performing large mutual fund in the world during his tenure. - Fidelity Investments; John Train, The New Money Masters (New York: Harper Business, 1989).

29. The "Buy What You Know" investment principle is attributed to Peter Lynch. - Peter Lynch, One Up on Wall Street (New York: Simon & Schuster, 1989).

30. Apple is among the most valuable companies in the world by market capitalization. - Source: companiesmarketcap.com or Bloomberg.

31. Johnson & Johnson has paid dividends for over 60 consecutive years. - Johnson & Johnson Investor Relations, dividend history, investor.jnj.com.

32. Walmart is the largest retailer in the world by revenue. - Fortune Global 500 list; Walmart corporate website, corporate.walmart.com.

33. Berkshire Hathaway Class A shares trade at over $720,000 per share. - Yahoo Finance or Bloomberg.

34. A P/E ratio of 15–20 is considered roughly average for a large U.S. company. - Based on historical S&P 500 P/E ratios. Source: Robert Shiller, CAPE Ratio data, econ.yale.edu; multpl.com/s-and-p-500-pe-ratio.

35. The S&P 500 is organized into 11 official sectors under the Global Industry Classification Standard (GICS). - MSCI and S&P Dow Jones Indices, GICS structure documentation.

36. In January 2021, GameStop's stock price rose from approximately $20 to nearly $500 in less than a month, driven in part by retail traders on Reddit's WallStreetBets forum. - U.S. Securities and Exchange Commission, Staff Report on Equity and Options Market Structure Conditions in Early 2021, October 2021; GameStop historical stock data.

37. During the COVID-19 pandemic, the S&P 500 dropped over 30% in approximately five weeks beginning in February 2020, bottomed in late March 2020, and recovered to new all-time highs by August 2020. - S&P 500 historical data. See also Source 20.

38. In early 2022, Netflix reported losing approximately 200,000 subscribers in a quarter when Wall Street had expected a gain of roughly 2.5 million. The stock dropped over 35% in a single day. - Netflix, Inc. Q1 2022 Earnings Report, April 19, 2022; analyst consensus estimates via Bloomberg or Refinitiv. Stock decline occurred April 20, 2022.

39. The Federal Reserve raised interest rates aggressively throughout 2022 and 2023 to combat inflation. During this period, the NASDAQ Composite Index declined over 30% from its peak. - Federal Reserve FOMC meeting minutes and rate decisions, federalreserve.gov; NASDAQ Composite historical data (peak November 2021 to trough).

40. The Federal Open Market Committee (FOMC) meets approximately every six weeks to set monetary policy. - Federal Reserve, FOMC meeting calendar, federalreserve.gov.

41. The Inflation Reduction Act of 2022 directed billions of dollars in federal spending toward clean energy, electric vehicles, and semiconductor manufacturing. - Inflation Reduction Act of 2022 (Pub. L. 117–169); White House factsheet, whitehouse.gov.

42. Russia invaded Ukraine on February 24, 2022, causing global energy prices to spike. - Associated Press and Reuters coverage, February 24, 2022.

43. Institutional investors account for approximately 70–80% of all trading volume on the U.S. stock market. - Pensions & Investments; SEC market structure studies. Note: Exact percentage varies by source and methodology.

44. Vanguard's S&P 500 index fund holds over $800 billion in assets under management. - Vanguard, fund factsheet for Vanguard 500 Index Fund (VFIAX).

45. In September 2023, the Federal Reserve announced it would hold interest rates steady. Apple rose approximately 1.5%, Bank of America dropped approximately 1%, and ExxonMobil was roughly flat on that trading day. - FOMC Statement, September 20, 2023; historical stock data for AAPL, BAC, and XOM on September 20, 2023. Verify exact percentage moves.

46. Apple's stock price rose from approximately $75 to over $180 between 2019 and 2021, forming a textbook uptrend. - Apple (AAPL) historical stock data, split-adjusted. Source: Yahoo Finance or TradingView.

47. Netflix's stock peaked near $700 in late 2021 and subsequently fell below $180 in 2022. - Netflix (NFLX) historical stock data. Source: Yahoo Finance or TradingView.

48. Amazon traded below approximately $145 through much of late 2023 before breaking through that resistance level in December 2023. - Amazon (AMZN) historical stock data. Source: Yahoo Finance or TradingView. Verify specific price level.

49. In January 2023, Tesla's RSI dropped below 30 as the stock fell from approximately $125 to below $110. Tesla subsequently rallied above $190 in the following weeks. - Tesla (TSLA) historical stock and RSI data, January–February 2023. Source: TradingView or Yahoo Finance.

50. NVIDIA surged past $500 in late 2023, driven by artificial intelligence enthusiasm, with its RSI climbing above 80. The stock subsequently pulled back approximately 10% before resuming its upward trend. - NVIDIA (NVDA) historical stock and RSI data, late 2023. Source: TradingView or Yahoo Finance.

51. Even the most successful professional traders typically win on only 40–50% of their trades. Profitability comes from ensuring winning trades are larger than losing trades. - Jack D. Schwager, Market Wizards (New York: New York Institute of Finance, 1989); Mark Minervini, Trade Like a Stock Market Wizard (New York: McGraw-Hill, 2013).

52. The greatest baseball hitters in the Hall of Fame had batting averages around .300, meaning they failed to get a hit 70% of the time. - Major League Baseball historical records, baseball-reference.com.

Selected Bibliography

Lynch, Peter. One Up on Wall Street. New York: Simon & Schuster, 1989.

Minervini, Mark. Trade Like a Stock Market Wizard. New York: McGraw-Hill, 2013.

Schroeder, Alice. The Snowball: Warren Buffett and the Business of Life. New York: Bantam Books, 2008.

Schwager, Jack D. Market Wizards: Interviews with Top Traders. New York: New York Institute of Finance, 1989.

Federal Reserve. FOMC Meeting Minutes and Statements. federalreserve.gov.

NYU Stern School of Business. Historical Returns on Stocks, Bonds and Bills. Damodaran Online.

S&P Dow Jones Indices. S&P 500 and DJIA Factsheets. spglobal.com.

U.S. Securities and Exchange Commission. Staff Report on Equity and Options Market Structure Conditions in Early 2021. October 2021.

U.S. Securities and Exchange Commission. Investor.gov Educational Resources. investor.gov.

ABOUT THE AUTHOR

Bhushan Polepally is a financial advisor, active stock trader, and holds an MBA in Finance. Over a career spanning more than fifteen years in the markets, he has navigated bull runs, bear markets, flash crashes, and everything in between - building a track record rooted in discipline, research, and risk management rather than luck or hype.

After years of advising clients who wished they had started investing decades earlier, Bhushan became passionate about closing the financial literacy gap at its source: young people. He created the *Paper Trading Boss Battles* series to give the next generation the education the current one never received - delivered in the gaming language they already speak.

When he's not analyzing markets or mentoring young investors, Bhushan can usually be found gaming - proving that the skills learned on the controller translate directly to the trading screen.

AUTHOR'S NOTE

If you're just starting out in trading and want to brush up on what you know or see where you stand, I suggest checking out the activities at the end of each chapter. Take a look at how you're approaching trading and see if there's anything you can improve. If you run into any challenges, dive back into the chapter to get a better grasp of the trading strategy and become a more confident and skilled trader.

Made in the USA
Monee, IL
08 November 2026

68063220R00123